SOCIAL DEVIANCY AND ADOLESCENT PERSONALITY

A UNIVERSITY OF
KENTUCKY STUDY

Social Deviancy and Adolescent Personality

AN ANALYTICAL STUDY
WITH THE MMPI

by

John C. Ball

GREENWOOD PRESS, PUBLISHERS
WESTPORT, CONNECTICUT

Library of Congress Cataloging in Publication Data

Ball, John Charles.
    Social deviancy and adolescent personality.

    (A University of Kentucky study)
    Includes bibliographical references.
    1. Adolescent psychology.   2. Deviant behavior.
3. Minnesota multiphasic personality inventory.
I. Title.
BF724.B28 1973   155.5   72-12308
ISBN 0-8371-6687-X

*The publication of this book has been made possible partly
through a grant from the Margaret Voorhies Haggin Trust,
established in memory of her husband, James Ben Ali Haggin.*

To the late

H. C. BREARLEY

FOREWORD

Less than two decades ago the first study of delinquency and personality characteristics in which the Minnesota Multiphasic Personality Inventory (MMPI) played a prominent role was published. This study, reported by Dora F. Capwell in 1945, produced results which suggested that the several scales of the MMPI differentiated significantly between groups of delinquent and nondelinquent girls.

The rather unusual aspect of the Capwell findings—unusual in the sense that they indicated that some of the MMPI scales seemed to have this discriminatory power—gave rise to a host of research projects employing the MMPI to contrast the personality characteristics of delinquent and nondelinquent boys and girls. With few exceptions these studies have substantiated the Capwell findings. In general, nondelinquent boys obtain scores showing them to be socially introverted, neurotic, and feminine in interests. Delinquent boys, contrastingly, tend to be socially aggressive, rebellious, cynical, negative, difficult, and expansive. Delinquent girls have distinguishing personality characteristics similar to those of delinquent boys.

The MMPI is a psychometric device which provides data on a variety of personality dimensions from a set of 550 items covering a wide range of topics. These items have usually been applied in the study of personality by the use of ten clinical scales and three validating scales which provide the standard MMPI personality profile. These profiles reveal the self-perception of the subject in relation to others in his social world as well as some of the various roles he plays. In other words, an individual's MMPI profile constitutes a personal and social self-evaluation.

Professor Ball further explores with the MMPI the interrelationships of behavior and personality. To this end he has made interesting and significant cross-sectional group comparisons of behavioral items and MMPI profile data. He has compared delinquents and nondelinquents, school achievers and nonachievers, white and Negro adolescents, low and high status high school students, adolescents who live in broken homes with those who do not, and adolescents who are rated by their teachers as maladjusted with those who are not. These comparisons are made in the hope of aiding in the development and use of more precise knowledge of the social and psychological factors associated with deviancy and conformity.

Professor Ball's findings again demonstrate that the MMPI is a useful instrument in the study of the personality patterns of nonconforming and conforming groups of adolescents.

STARKE R. HATHAWAY
ELIO D. MONACHESI

ACKNOWLEDGMENTS

I am indebted to Vice President Herman E. Spivey of the University of Tennessee for his encouragement to initiate this study. The assistance of Austin T. Turk was invaluable in planning the project and collecting the data.

It is a pleasure to thank F. D. Wilkinson and O. A. Adams, as well as the many teachers and more numerous students, for generously contributing their time and effort to this project.

Robert Hammond, former superintendent of Kentucky Village, was most helpful in facilitating the collection of information at the training school.

Financial support for this study was provided by the Kentucky Research Foundation of the University of Kentucky. I also wish to acknowledge assistance received from the Department of Sociology and the Computer Center, both of the University of Kentucky.

Miss Rosa Lena Brumfield assisted the project continually in varied ways and undertook the major secretarial tasks. In this regard, thanks are also due Mrs. Nancy Chairatana, Miss Cynthia Allen, Miss Alice Simpson, and Mrs. Emily Cottrell.

Lastly, I wish to thank Dr. S. R. Hathaway and Professor Elio D. Monachesi for their interest in this study and for their many helpful suggestions.

JOHN C. BALL

CONTENTS

TABLES, LISTS OF CODES, FIGURES

1

THE STUDY OF SOCIAL DEVIANCY
AND PERSONALITY

*T*HE PURPOSE of this study is to trace the relationship of personality to social deviancy among adolescents. In particular, the association of delinquency, minority group status, low socioeconomic status, broken homes, and failure in school with personality patterns among Kentucky boys and girls of high school age is the subject of analysis.

The problem of ascertaining the relationship of adolescent personality to various types of behavior and environmental conditions is one of far-reaching significance in the behavioral sciences. It is an important problem because we are interested in determining how personality develops. In order to accomplish this, two research approaches seem necessary:

1. Delineation of personality patterns to be found within the various segments of the youthful population. The emphasis here is upon cross-sectional studies.
2. Determination of the complex of influences and factors which produce change in the personality of children. Longitudinal studies which trace the development in personality over a period of years would be required in this instance.

These two approaches to the study of youthful personality—and behavior—are interrelated. In the first case, the objective is to establish the distribution of personality patterns in the population and to relate these characteristics to such personal and background factors as shyness, aggressiveness, intelligence, health, broken homes, and school failure. In these studies common personality patterns found among the nation's youth are described and variations from the typical delineated. Thus, the mild rebelliousness and considerable energy among adolescents of high school age have been substantiated by objective personality measurement. Among juvenile delinquents, the dominance of an antisocial personality type has been consistently reported.[1]

Secondly, longitudinal studies will build upon our knowledge of general population characteristics by tracing more precise relationships between personality characteristics and influencing factors. It seems likely, however, that these more carefully controlled studies of small groups over considerable time periods will be more definitive if undertaken when the major personality patterns and variations from these patterns have been established by exploratory studies of the first type.

[1] Starke R. Hathaway and Elio D. Monachesi, eds., *Analyzing and Predicting Juvenile Delinquency with the MMPI* (Minneapolis: University of Minnesota Press, 1953); Starke R. Hathaway, Elio D. Monachesi and Lawrence A. Young, "Delinquency Rates and Personality," *Journal of Criminal Law, Criminology and Police Science,* Vol. 50 (February, 1960), pp. 433-440.

The present study follows the first of the two approaches described. Its objective is the delineation of personality patterns within various segments of a high school population. Personal, family, and community factors which may influence personality patterns are considered with a view to determining which of these is associated with satisfactory and which with unsatisfactory personality characteristics. Attention is focused upon such specific questions as: What effect do broken homes have upon the personality of high school students? Is there less personality maladjustment among girls than boys? Are incarcerated juvenile delinquents different in personality from public school students who have committed delinquent acts? Are Negro boys or girls more successful in academic competition in an integrated high school? To what extent is academic performance related to personality traits and to socioeconomic status? What types of students do high school teachers consider to be maladjusted?

SOCIAL DEVIANCY

In answering these and other questions pertaining to adolescent personality and behavior, the concept of social deviancy is employed. Social deviancy is defined as behavior or status which is contrary to existing social norms of what is right and desirable. It is, in American society, deviation from middle class expectations and goals. Hence, delinquency, academic failure, and being rated by teachers as maladjusted in personality are regarded as deviance. In addition, low socioeconomic status, residence in a broken home, or membership in a segregated minority group may be regarded as deviant. For the purposes of this study, all of these are termed social deviancy.

It seems appropriate to mention the limitations of the social deviancy formulation as well as to indicate its usefulness. The main source of likely confusion is semantic. It is imperative to note that the term social deviance is not being employed to make a value judgment. It is not main-

3

tained that the middle class norms are right and correct in any ultimate sense. There are, of course, some groups and societies not worth adjusting to, and genius perhaps more commonly than not is at variance with middle class norms.

The social deviancy approach has the advantage of providing a single framework within which diverse types of adolescent behavior and environment may be conveniently related to personality patterns. It permits multiple comparisons among various groups of subjects without the attribution of fundamental inferiority or superiority. The extent to which high school boys and girls are deviant in personality or behavior is a question for empirical determination, not categorical definition.

THE RESEARCH DESIGN

The study is a cross-sectional multi-group comparison of personality and behavioral interrelations. The cake is cut in as many ways as is feasible. Delinquents are compared with nondelinquents, white with Negro students, subjects of higher socioeconomic status with those of lower status, adolescents from broken homes with those from stable families, high achievers with low achievers, and those rated by teachers as maladjusted with those not so rated. The groups are analyzed and compared using background factors of age, residence, intelligence quotient, employment, and educational retardation, as well as the selection factors of delinquency, race, socioeconomic status, family composition, school achievement, and teachers' ratings. Included in the group personality comparisons are Minnesota Multiphasic Personality Inventory data on test-taking attitudes, profile elevation, first clinical scale in code, and code configuration. Individual as well as group profiles are presented.

All in all, the purpose of this differential cross-sectional analysis is ascertainment of relative personality and behavioral similarities and differences *within* the adolescent population. As Sherif has said, "The task is to go beyond the

4

general statement that everything is related to everything else within the frame of reference and laboriously to vary this factor now, that factor later, with the ultimate aim of finding the relative *weights* for each and finally, expressing the relations in short-cut expressions."[2] Inkeles has observed in this regard that "we need to know not only the systems of statuses but also the distribution of personality characteristics in the population at large and among the incumbents of particular roles."[3]

With respect to MMPI analysis, this design has particular implications. It is frequently assumed that a given group of subjects—high achievers or delinquents, for example—possess a definite MMPI profile. In the present study, differential group comparisons demonstrate that various group personality profiles emerge from within the same sample, even though the individual MMPI profiles remain unchanged. The implications of this finding are far-reaching and suggest the limitation of one-factor analysis. Thus, in studies which compare mean scale scores of two groups, there may be the inference that the observed differences are the principal ones, whereas other factors may in fact be of greater import. This methodological problem has been neglected in the MMPI literature, although attention has been drawn to the need for studies from such additional populations as racial and religious groups.[4]

SUBJECTS

The subjects were 262 Kentucky adolescents. Of this number 108 were ninth grade public school boys and 116 were ninth grade public school girls. The remaining 38 subjects were

[2] John H. Rohrer and Muzafer Sherif, eds., *Social Psychology at the Crossroads* (New York: Harper and Brothers, 1951), p. 5.

[3] Alex Inkeles, "Personality and Social Structure," *Sociology Today*, ed. Robert K. Merton, Leonard Broom and Leonard S. Cottrell, Jr. (New York: Basic Books, 1959), p. 262.

[4] W. Grant Dahlstrom and George Schlager Welsh, eds., *An MMPI Handbook* (Minneapolis: University of Minnesota Press, 1960), p. 120.

incarcerated juvenile delinquents of whom 20 were male and 18 female.

Each of the two towns from which the public school samples were selected had a population in 1960 between 10,000 and 19,000. With respect to occupational distribution and median family income the two towns were similar to other urban areas of comparable size in Kentucky. From 13 to 17 percent of their 1960 populations were Negro.

The two school systems ranked in the upper one-fifth of the 215 school districts in Kentucky with regard to mean salary of teachers in 1958-1959. The school systems were, however, in the same salary range as other towns of comparable population. It is pertinent to note that the demographic and educational data reveal striking contrasts between urban and rural areas throughout Kentucky, so that it would be hazardous to generalize with respect to the entire state. For example, in 1958-1959 mean salaries of teachers by school districts ranged from somewhat over $5,000 to less than $2,000.

In each town the entire ninth grade of the city schools was included, with the exception of students absent on the day the MMPI was administered. The 21 absentee students constituted some 9 percent of the total ninth grade enrollment in both schools.

The ninth grade was selected because previous research in Minnesota had indicated that the MMPI could be successfully administered to students at this early grade level. It was considered advisable to secure as young a group as possible, since research has demonstrated the early etiology of most deviant behavior. Among boys, delinquent acts have usually commenced by age ten to fifteen.[5]

To secure a delinquent population for comparison, it was decided to include a group of incarcerated delinquents at the State Training School, as well as to compare public school students with and without records of delinquency.

[5] Sophia M. Robison, *Juvenile Delinquency* (New York: Henry Holt and Company, 1960), chapter 4.

6

For the incarcerated delinquents, the limiting selection factor was ability to comprehend the 550 MMPI items. Enrollment at the State Training School on March 6, 1958, was 404 juveniles. Of these 302 were boys and 102 girls. This seemingly large population, however, was markedly retarded in academic achievement and considerably below average in intellectual endowment. The average I.Q. has been reported in the 75-80 range for the institution.[6] Educational retardation associated with reading deficiency or illiteracy was undoubtedly even more important as a restriction at the reformatory school since there were only some 38 delinquents in the eighth grade or above. Grade placement in the reformatory school was effected by use of standard achievement tests. As a result, retardation at the Training School was even more marked than it had been before incarceration. The contention of the principal that achievement at the Training School was equal or superior to that of comparable public school grades was supported by the capacity of the delinquents to understand and complete the MMPI. The test population of 38 subjects included, then, all incarcerated delinquents who were deemed capable of comprehending the MMPI items.

The 38 incarcerated delinquents selected came from 17 counties, but 76 percent of this incarcerated group came from the 16 most urban of the 120 counties in Kentucky. The delinquents, then, were disproportionally from the urban and metropolitan areas. It may be noted, in this connection, that the two towns from which the public school samples were drawn were included in the 16 most urban counties of Kentucky.

DATA COLLECTED

Each student completed an occupational information sheet at the time the MMPI was administered. This included

[6] Frank Kodman, Jr., *et al.*, "Some Implications of Hearing Defective Juvenile Delinquents," *Exceptional Children*, Vol. 25 (October, 1958), p. 54.

questions regarding his own and his parents' employment and whether or not his parents were living together. Data on age, race, nativity, intelligence quotient, educational retardation, and school achievement were obtained from school or institutional records. In addition, each homeroom teacher was asked to evaluate his students with respect to "personality adjustment" and evidences of antisocial attitudes or behavior. Information on delinquency among the public school students was secured from court records, policemen and other officials. The offenses perpetrated by the incarcerated delinquents were taken from institutional records.

For the most part, the above information was obtained with only negligible or expected omissions. Reasons for omission included such circumstances as inability to ascertain previous school achievement because the students had recently transferred, or inadequate information upon which to establish socioeconomic status. The principal exception was that I.Q. records were quite incomplete in one of the schools. Otherwise, the background data were reasonably complete.

ADMINISTRATION OF THE MMPI

The complete booklet form of the MMPI was administered under standard conditions by trained personnel. Time required to complete the 566 items[7] varied from one to three hours, with most students finishing in under two hours. Each student wrote his name on the MMPI answer sheet in the appropriate place. The author agrees with Meehl and Hathaway concerning the undesirability of administering anonymous or apparently anonymous personality tests.[8]

Criteria employed in rendering profiles invalid were

[7] The full booklet form and the machine scored answer sheet contain 550 different items; 16 items are repeated to facilitate machine scoring.

[8] Paul E. Meehl and Starke R. Hathaway, "The K Factor as a Suppressor Variable in the Minnesota Multiphasic Personality Inventory," *Journal of Applied Psychology*, Vol. 30 (October, 1946), p. 528.

somewhat more stringent than is commonly the case. As is usual, an L score of 10 or more, an F score of 16 or more, or a ? score of 100 or greater was considered indicative of invalid responses.[9] In addition, an F-K score of 9 or more was used as a measure of invalidity. The F-K criterion of invalidity is suggested by Gough as being more discriminating than the F scale separately.[10] Employing these criteria, 28 profiles were classified as invalid.

The ten clinical and four validity scales were scored in the customary manner; K corrections have been applied to five of the clinical scales throughout the analysis. The clinical scales are reported in T-scores, but raw scores are reported for the validity scales.[11] Welsh's extended coding procedure is employed in the comparison and analysis of MMPI profiles.[12]

THE MMPI: AN OVERVIEW

The Minnesota Multiphasic Personality Inventory consists of 550 brief statements of personal experiences, feelings, and attitudes. Included are items which refer to the subject's general health, bodily functions, habits, family relationships, occupational and educational experiences, sexual, religious, political and general social attitudes, affective and compulsive states, illusions, phobias, morale, masculinity-feminity, and dissimulation tendencies. Separate card and booklet forms

[9] S. R. Hathaway and J. C. McKinley, *Minnesota Multiphasic Personality Inventory Manual* (rev.; New York: The Psychological Corporation, 1951).

[10] Harrison G. Gough, "The F Minus K Dissimulation Index for the Minnesota Multiphasic Personality Inventory," *Journal of Consulting Psychology*, Vol. 14 (September-October, 1950), pp. 408-413.

[11] In the present case, it seemed advisable to report raw ?, L, F, and K scores since much of the pertinent previous research followed this procedure; these scores can, of course, be easily transformed into T-scores for other purposes.

[12] George S. Welsh, "An Extension of Hathaway's MMPI Profile Coding System," *Journal of Consulting Psychology*, Vol. 12 (September-October, 1948), pp. 343-344. For a further explanation of this procedure see below.

are available for individual or group administration of the inventory. In answering the items the subject is asked to indicate whether the statement is true or false as it applies to him.

The MMPI contains four validity and ten clinical scales in its present standard form.[13] Each scale (except the "Cannot Say" or "?" scale) consists of a number of specified items scored in a prescribed manner. The scales were empirically derived; items were not selected on the basis of face validity.[14]

The validity scales—?, L, F, and K—were designed to afford a measure of the subject's test-taking attitudes. The Cannot Say score (often designated ? score) consists of the number of items left blank. Excessive omissions preclude meaningful interpretation of the inventory; hence, the Cannot Say score is ordinarily the first one checked. In addition to providing a gross validity measure, the Cannot Say score has also been regarded as affording a measure of other more subtle test-taking attitudes.[15] The L scale contains items which indicate whether or not the subject is attempting to place himself in an unusually favorable light. A high L score is an indication that the subject is "faking-good." The third validity scale, F, is the obverse of L; it indicates whether or not the subject is "faking-bad," or attempting to place

[13] *Booklet for the Minnesota Multiphasic Personality Inventory* (New York: The Psychological Corporation, 1943).

[14] S. R. Hathaway and J. C. McKinley, "A Multiphasic Personality Schedule (Minnesota): I. Construction of the Schedule," *Journal of Psychology*, Vol. 10 (October, 1940), pp. 249-254; J. C. McKinley, S. R. Hathaway and P. E. Meehl, "The Minnesota Multiphasic Personality Inventory: VI. The K Scale," *Journal of Consulting Psychology*, Vol. 12 (January-February, 1948), pp. 20-31; Paul E. Meehl, "The Dynamics of 'Structured' Personality Tests," *Journal of Clinical Psychology*, Vol. 1 (October, 1945), pp. 296-303; W. Grant Dahlstrom, "Research in Clinical Psychology: Factor Analytic Contributions," *Journal of Clinical Psychology*, Vol. 13 (July, 1957), pp. 211-220.

[15] John C. Ball and Donna Carroll, "Analysis of MMPI Cannot Say Scores in an Adolescent Population," *Journal of Clinical Psychology*, Vol. 16 (January, 1960), pp. 30-31.

himself in an unusually unfavorable light. The K scale was originally devised as a Correction Scale to improve the discriminatory power of the clinical scales by correcting for dissimulation. It has also been found, however, to provide a measure of test-taking attitudes.

The MMPI includes nine clinical scales. These are (1) the Hypochondriasis Scale—Hs, (2) Depression Scale—D, (3) Hysteria Scale—Hy, (4) Psychopathic Deviate Scale—Pd, (5) Masculinity-Femininity Scale—Mf, (6) Paranoia Scale— Pa, (7) Psychasthenia Scale—Pt, (8) Schizophrenia Scale— Sc, and (9) Hypomania Scale—Ma. These scales are commonly referred to by the abbreviation indicated or by number. Thus, the Depression Scale is referred to as the D scale, or as scale 2. In addition to the above nine scales, a tenth has been added on the standard profile sheets. It is the Social Introversion Scale—Si—and is numbered "0."[16] For a brief description of the clinical and validity scales, see Table 1.

High scores on any of the clinical scales among patient groups are considered indicative of psychiatric classification. In nonclinical groups, the interpretation of scores is attenuated or modified to the extent that moderately high scores (T-score 60-70) are not necessarily indicative of the classic psychiatric condition designated by the scale. Adolescents commonly score somewhat higher than adults, but below clinical groups, on Pd and Ma. This higher score of adolescents is not evidence that the subjects are psychopathic or hypomanic. Among adolescents, moderately high Pd and Ma scores appear to delineate mild unconventionality and rebellion against social norms as well as somewhat excessive energy and enthusiasm.

Standard scores for the various scales have been derived. The T-score 50 point represents the normal population mean.

[16] For information concerning the construction of the Si scale see Lewis E. Drake, "A Social I. E. Scale for the Minnesota Multiphasic Personality Inventory," *Journal of Applied Psychology*, Vol. 30 (February, 1946), pp. 51-54.

11

The 45 to 54 range is considered normal or nonelevated. T-scores of 55 to 70 on particular scales are suggestive of moderate elevation, while scores of 70 and above are regarded as indicative of pathology. A score of 70 is two standard deviations above the adult population norm.

Table 1. Brief Description of MMPI Scales

Scale No.	Abbr.	Clinical Manifestation or Description	In a normal or nonclinical population, high scores indicative of:
1	Hs	Hypochondriasis	Undue *concern with bodily health*; tired, ill, inactive
2	D	Depression	*Depressed*; unhappy, serious, low morale
3	Hy	Hysteria	Problems solved by *physical symptoms*; ill, under stress
4	Pd	Psychopathic Deviate	*Asocial, rebellious*; aggressive, immature
5	Mf	Masculinity-Feminity	*Interests of opposite sex*; roughness for females, sensitivity for males
6	Pa	Paranoia	*Suspiciousness*; oversensitive socially, rigid personality
7	Pt	Psychasthenia	*Fears and inferiority feelings*; compulsive behavior, dependent
8	Sc	Schizophrenia	*Disorganized thought and behavior*; lacking social grace
9	Ma	Hypomania	*Overactive* in thought and behavior; expansive, transient enthusiasms
0	Si	Social Introversion	*Withdrawn socially*; self-conscious, shy
	?	Cannot Say Scale	Meager literacy or defensiveness (score is number of omitted items)
	L	Lie Scale	Naive attempt at "faking-good"
	F	F Scale	Self-deprecation, or "faking-bad"
	K	Correction Scale	Subtle attempt at "faking-good"

Increasingly, research with the MMPI has been directed toward ascertainment of personality configurations or patterns. Indeed, it is not so much the particular scores received which are significant, but the relationship among the scale scores, as reflected in the MMPI profile. Delinquents, for example, usually peak on scale 4—Pd. In addition to the standard profile, several coding systems have been devised to further configural analysis. One of the most widely used is that of Welsh. In this coding procedure, the 10 clinical

12

scales are ranked from high to low and the respective elevations designated. The validity scales follow the clinical scales and are coded separately. The delinquent boy's code 2′47-89/01 356: L-KF/?: delineates a profile in which scale 2, Depression, is the highest and scale 6, Paranoia, is the lowest. The apostrophe following 2 denotes the 70 to 80 T-score range, the dash after 47 the 60 to 70 elevation, the diagonal or slash 50 to 60, and the colon the 40 to 50 range. Thus, scale 2 is between 70 and 79, scales 4 and 7 are in the 60 through 69 range, scales 8 and 9 are in the 50 through 59 range, and so forth. The underlined scales, as 89, are scales with the same T-score or within one T-score of each other. This coding procedure permits a ready description and analysis of the profile configuration.

2

DELINQUENCY AND PERSONALITY

$\mathcal{I}$N THE United States delinquency is one of the most widespread and frequent types of deviant behavior among adolescents. Although the seriousness and frequency of offenses vary between rural and metropolitan areas, by eighteen years of age some 35 percent of the male population have had their names recorded by the police or courts.[1]

In Part I of this chapter, 34 incarcerated juvenile delinquents are compared with 200 ninth grade public school students with respect to background characteristics and personality profiles. The 28 subjects with invalid MMPI profiles were not included in the present study. A separate comparison of those public school students with and those without records of delinquency is then undertaken in Part II. This is a subgroup analysis of the 200 public school students—or nondelinquents.

1

COMPARISON OF INCARCERATED DELINQUENTS WITH PUBLIC SCHOOL STUDENTS

The 34 incarcerated delinquents selected were about one year older than the public school students (Table 2). The range in age for both groups was from 13 through 18 years, but 88 percent of the delinquents and 94 percent of the nondelinquents were 14, 15, or 16 years old.

There were 31 Negroes in the nondelinquent public school population, none among the delinquents. (The reformatory population of 405 juveniles included 78 Negro boys and girls, 12 of whom were in the eighth and ninth grades. The Negro group was not included in the delinquent sample because the two groups were segregated in living quarters and education.) The delinquents and nondelinquents were similar in nativity—88 percent of each group having been born in Kentucky.

With respect to intelligence quotient, the delinquents and nondelinquents were quite similar. This similarity was due to the selection of the delinquents from the upper grades at the reformatory and does not reflect the markedly lower I.Q. of the entire institutional population.

The I.Q. data were incomplete and of limited comparability. Among the nondelinquents, no intelligence test scores were available for 54 of the 200 students. For those tested, different instruments were used, the two most common

[1] Starke R. Hathaway, Elio D. Monachesi and Lawrence A. Young, "Delinquency Rates and Personality," *Journal of Criminal Law, Criminology and Police Science,* Vol. 50 (February, 1960), p. 435; Thomas P. Monahan, "On the Incidence of Delinquency," *Social Forces,* Vol. 39 (October, 1960), pp. 66-72.

Table 2. Age, Nativity, Intelligence Quotient, School Grades, Educational Retardation, After-School Employment, Family Composition, and Socioeconomic Status of Delinquents and Nondelinquents by Sex[a]

Group	N	Mean Age	Kentucky Nativity, Percent	Mean I.Q.	Grade Average	Retarded in school Percent	Percent Employed Part-Time	Broken Homes Percent	Lower Class, Percent
Delinquent Boys	19	16.0**	94.7	99.4	4.5 (C)	78.9**	26.3	57.9**	57.9**
Nondelinquent Boys	95	15.0	83.2	103.7	4.5 (C)	34.0	29.5	12.6	28.4
Delinquent Girls	15	15.8**	80.0	99.3	5.1 (C+)	66.7**	26.7	26.7	46.7*
Nondelinquent Girls	105	14.8	91.3	104.2	5.1 (C+)	17.1	9.5	20.0	23.8

[a] Difference between delinquent and nondelinquent boys, or girls, significant at level of: *P < .05; **P < .01. No test of significance applied to I.Q. data. For reason see text.

being Kuhlman-Anderson and Wechsler-Bellevue. Among the delinquents I.Q.'s were available for 32 of the 34 subjects. These scores were obtained from the psychologist at the institution who used the Otis Quick Scoring Mental Abilities Test. For the incarcerated delinquents, then, the I.Q. data were considerably more satisfactory than those obtained for the public school students. All in all, however, it seems likely that the test scores provide, despite the limitations mentioned, a fair indication of comparative intelligence for the several groups.

The delinquents were markedly more retarded in grade placement than the nondelinquents, 79 percent of the delinquent boys and 67 percent of the delinquent girls being retarded one or more years while only 34 percent of the nondelinquent boys and 17 percent of the girls were similarly retarded. This difference was doubtless accentuated by the fact that grade placement in the reformatory school was on the basis of standard achievement tests. All of the public school students were in the ninth grade. Among the delinquents, eight boys and six girls were in the tenth grade, and seven boys and three girls were in the eighth grade; the remaining delinquents were ninth graders. When retardation of two or more years is considered, this contrast in academic achievement is still more revealing; 47 percent of the delinquent group was so retarded in contrast with 4 percent of the nondelinquents. Boys were more retarded in grade placement than girls in both the delinquent and nondelinquent groups.

The recent achievement records of the delinquents and nondelinquents were quite similar. School achievement was computed for each student on the basis of the previous semester's average letter grade. For the delinquents, this referred to grades received at the school in the reformatory. In both groups, the girls received higher grades than the boys.

Of the nondelinquent boys 29.5 percent held jobs, as did 9.5 percent of the girls. Among the delinquents, 26.3

Table 3. Number of Years Delinquent and Nondelinquent Students Were Retarded in Grade Placement

Years Retarded	Boys				Girls			
	Delinquent		Nondelinquent		Delinquent		Nondelinquent	
	Number	Percent	Number	Percent	Number	Percent	Number	Percent
0	4	21.1	62	66.0	5	33.3	87	82.9
1	6	31.6	26	27.7	3	20.0	16	15.2
2	6	31.6	4	4.3	3	20.0	2	1.9
3 or 4	3	15.8	2	2.1	4	26.7		
Total	19	100.0	94*	100.0	15	100.0	105	100.0

* One nondelinquent boy omitted from tabulation due to absence of birth data.
  Difference between delinquents and nondelinquents in grade retardation: Boys $X^2 = 25.57$, $P < .001$; Girls $X^2 = 39.66$, $P < .001$.
  Note: Underline of last digit in total percent figure indicates that addition of the above column does not precisely equal 100.0 due to rounding error.

percent of the boys and 26.7 percent of the girls were employed before incarceration. Of these employed delinquents, however, approximately half (60.0 percent of the boys, 50.0 percent of the girls) had left school prior to incarceration. Delinquent boys and girls worked longer hours than did the nondelinquents. Among those employed, the mean hours worked per week were 12.7 for the nondelinquent boys, 13.0 for the nondelinquent girls, 32.5 for the delinquent boys and 40.0 for the delinquent girls. Eighteen nondelinquent boys were engaged in delivery jobs, including paper routes, seven were employed as clerks or helpers in stores or service stations, two worked at home for their families, and one was unclassified as to type of employment. Among the nondelinquent girls, four were baby sitters, four clerked, and two held office jobs. Two delinquent boys were engaged before incarceration in delivery work, two were helpers, and one was unclassified. All four delinquent girls were employed before incarceration as clerks or helpers, two of these as "car-hops" in drive-in restaurants.

Of the nondelinquent boys 12.6 percent were from homes broken by divorce, separation or death; 20.0 percent of the nondelinquent girls, 57.9 percent of the delinquent boys, and 26.7 percent of the delinquent girls were from such homes.[2]

In Table 4 the socioeconomic status of the four groups is indicated on a seven-point scale from high to low on *The Minnesota Scale for Paternal Occupations.*[3] Of the delin-

[2] The prevalence of broken homes among the delinquent boys is in accord with the results of previous studies. The lesser proportion of delinquent girls from broken homes, however, is rather surprising in view of the usual findings that female juvenile delinquents more frequently than male come from broken homes. H. Ashley Weeks, "Male and Female Broken Home Rates by Types of Delinquency," *American Sociological Review*, Vol. 5 (August, 1940), pp. 601-609; William W. Wattenberg and Frank Saunders, "Sex Differences Among Juvenile Offenders," *Sociology and Social Research*, Vol. 39 (August-September, 1954), pp. 24-31.

[3] *The Minnesota Scale for Paternal Occupations* (Minneapolis: University of Minnesota, Institute of Child Welfare, n. d.).

Table 4. Socioeconomic Status of Delinquent and Nondelinquent Students as Ranked on the Minnesota Scale for Paternal Occupations

Class	Socio-economic Status	Boys				Girls			
		Nondelinquent		Delinquent		Nondelinquent		Delinquent	
		Number	Percent	Number	Percent	Number	Percent	Number	Percent
Upper	1	8	8.4			7	6.9		
	2	12	12.6			12	11.9		
Middle	3	20	21.1	2	10.5	24	23.8		
	4	1	1.1	1	5.3	4	4.0		
	5	27	28.4	5	26.3	30	29.7	8	53.3
Lower	6	14	14.7	4	21.1	19	18.8	4	26.7
	7	13	13.7	7	36.8	5	5.0	3	20.0
	Total	95	100.0	19	100.0	101	100.0	15	100.0

* Four cases omitted due to lack of data pertaining to status.

Difference in socioeconomic status of delinquents and nondelinquents: Boys X^2 = 8.36, P < .02; Girls X^2 = 5.42, P < .10.

quent population, 91.2 percent were in the three lowest classes. By contrast, only 55.1 percent of the nondelinquent students were in these three classes. The distribution of nondelinquents within the seven socioeconomic levels follows general demographic expectations. The paucity of subjects in status 4, farmers, is due to the fact that the two public high schools are in urban areas. There is reason to believe, however, that the nondelinquent distribution is of somewhat higher socioeconomic level (more students in middle and upper classes, fewer in lower classes) than the general population of these Kentucky towns.

The records of the delinquent boys showed larceny (6), burglary (4), auto theft (3), robbery (2), and assault, attempted rape, incorrigibility, and neglect (1 each). The delinquent girls had records indicating sexual promiscuity (10), incorrigibility (3), and larceny and truancy (1 each).[4] The offense named was the latest charged and the one which resulted in the present incarceration. While this list indicates the types of offenses committed, it does not suggest the long history of delinquency which usually preceded incarceration. The case histories reveal a pattern of repeated theft and vandalism for the boys with a corresponding history of incorrigibility and sexual promiscuity for the girls.

The most noticeable differences, then, between the delinquent and nondelinquent populations were with respect to educational retardation, socioeconomic status, and family composition. The delinquents were more retarded in grade placement, were from lower socioeconomic strata, and, particularly among the boys, were more often from broken homes. In addition, the delinquents are characterized by long histories of persistent offenses.

---

[4] For a further delineation of a similar sample of delinquent girls from the same institution see: John C. Ball and Nell Logan, "Early Sexual Behavior of Lower-Class Delinquent Girls," *Journal of Criminal Law, Criminology and Police Science*, Vol. 51 (July-August, 1960), pp. 209-214.

Table 5. MMPI Mean Scale Scores, Standard Deviations, and t Values of Incarcerated Juvenile Delinquents and Public School Students[a]

Scale	Boys					Girls				
	Delinquent N=19		Nondelinquent N=95		t-Test	Delinquent N=15		Nondelinquent N=105		t-Test
	Mean	S.D.	Mean	S.D.		Mean	S.D.	Mean	S.D.	
?	5.3	9.73	6.7	11.02	0.538	1.1	1.34	3.1	8.28	0.935
L	3.7	1.66	3.5	2.05	0.334	2.8	1.17	4.0	2.03	2.251*
F	6.6	4.04	6.0	3.41	0.743	9.1	4.77	5.8	3.45	3.216**
K	14.3	5.57	11.9	4.53	1.989*	10.2	3.21	13.0	4.80	2.166*
1 (Hs)	52.9	7.20	51.3	9.54	0.723	50.0	8.33	49.5	8.45	0.231
2 (D)	57.3	10.19	54.0	11.52	1.146	49.3	11.35	50.9	8.25	0.641
3 (Hy)	53.0	7.80	52.8	6.65	0.127	54.3	9.10	52.8	9.00	0.596
4 (Pd)	69.9	7.40	59.7	9.10	4.547**	75.7	11.46	61.1	10.30	5.044**
5 (Mf)	57.5	11.01	53.5	7.99	1.831	55.2	10.63	51.6	8.57	1.473
6 (Pa)	58.2	9.69	54.3	8.77	1.724	65.3	8.74	56.0	9.67	3.464**
7 (Pt)	60.0	8.09	58.3	10.28	0.659	56.5	9.58	57.2	8.48	0.298
8 (Sc)	64.4	12.01	59.3	10.23	1.894	69.3	12.61	59.9	9.52	3.418**
9 (Ma)	63.8	9.88	62.3	11.00	0.576	72.6	7.35	60.4	9.63	4.682**
0 (Si)	50.0	9.49	53.5	8.92	1.547	50.8	9.38	52.8	8.05	0.857

[a] Validity scales are reported in mean raw scores, clinical scales in mean T-scores. K corrections have been applied to scales 1, 4, 7, 8, and 9. Significance of difference between means: *P < .05; **P < .01.

22

The greatest differences between the delinquent and non-delinquent boys were on scales 4 and 8—psychopathic deviate and schizophrenia. In particular, the Pd scale was markedly elevated among the delinquents; this difference was statistically significant. The delinquent boys were somewhat higher on scales 2, 5, and 6, although the differences were not significant.

The delinquent boys also had higher scores on the three validity scales, L, F, and K. These differences do not appear, however, despite the statistically significant difference in K scores, to indicate any difference in test-taking attitudes between the two groups.

The delinquent girls had significantly higher mean scores on scales 4, 6, 8, and 9—Pd, Pa, Sc, and Ma. On each of these four scales, the delinquents were some ten points higher in mean scores than the nondelinquents; these differences are significant at the .001 level.

On the validity scales, the delinquent girls had lower scores on L and K than the nondelinquents, but higher F scores. Such scores suggest less defensiveness or a greater willingness to put oneself in an unfavorable light on the part of the female delinquents. The lower L score in particular suggests greater candor on the part of the delinquent girls.

Use of MMPI coding makes it possible to compare and contrast scale configurations as well as separate scales, and thus to arrive at an interpretation of the relationship of personality variables. The MMPI codes for the delinquent boys, delinquent girls, nondelinquent boys, and nondelinquent girls were as follows:

	Boys	Girls
Delinquent	4 89 7-652 31 0/ FK/L?:	49'86-7 53 01/2: F-KL?:
Nondelinquent	9-487 62503 1/ F/LK ?:	49-8 76 30 52/1: F KL/?:

23

24

Table 6. Number of Clinical Scales With T-Scores of 70 or Above for Delinquent and Nondelinquent Students

Number of Scales 70 or above	Boys				Girls				Total	
	Delinquent		Nondelinquent		Delinquent		Nondelinquent			
	Number	Percent	Number	Percent	Number	Percent	Number	Percent	Number	Percent
0	2	10.5	43	45.3	3	20.0	60	57.1	108	46.2
1	10	52.6	27	28.4	2	13.3	20	19.0	59	25.2
2	3	15.8	10	10.5	5	33.3	14	13.3	32	13.7
3	1	5.3	10	10.5	1	6.7	5	4.8	17	7.3
4	2	10.5	4	4.2			2	1.9	8	3.4
5	1	5.3	1	1.1	3	20.0	4	3.8	9	3.8
6					1	6.7			1	0.4
7										
8										
9										
10										
Total	19	100.0	95	100.0	15	100.0	105	100.0	234	100.0

Difference in profile elevation between delinquents and nondelinquents: Boys $X^2 = 11.04$, $P < .05$; Girls $X^2 = 14.01$, $P < .01$.

The MMPI code of the delinquent boys is characterized by the prominence of scale 4. Next in prominence are scales 8 and 9, followed by 7. This pattern suggests the prominence of the schizoid and manic tendencies as well as the lack of confidence frequently expressed by high Pt scores. The neurotic scales 1, 2, and 3 are toward the lower end of the code, as is common, but the higher D is worth noting. It seems probable that this depression is a result of incarceration.[5] The F score is somewhat high. This slight elevation of F probably reflects some difficulty in comprehension of items, rather than an inclination toward faking-bad.

The delinquent girls' code is characterized by the prominence of both 9 and 4. Next in importance are scales 8 and 6, suggesting sensitivity in addition to schizoid trends. The lower scores on scales 7 and 2 would appear to reflect somewhat more self-confidence and less depression on the part of the delinquent girls than among the delinquent boys. At the same time, the validity scales present evidence of less defensiveness in test-taking attitude on the part of the delinquent girls, as seen in the high F combined with a low K and L.[6] Contrasted with the boys, the delinquent girls appear to be more energetic and rigid, less depressed and defensive. Statistically significant (t test, $P<.05$) differences in mean scale scores between the delinquent boys and the delinquent girls were found on scales K, 2, 6, and 9. The boys were higher on the K and D scales, the girls on Pa and Ma. (These means, but not the t values, are presented in Table 5.)

[5] Similar findings pertaining to depression are reported by Monachesi. He likewise found incarcerated boys to be more depressed than girls. Elio D. Monachesi, "The Personality Patterns of Juvenile Delinquents as Indicated by the MMPI," *Analyzing and Predicting Juvenile Delinquency with the MMPI*, Starke R. Hathaway and Elio D. Monachesi, eds. (Minneapolis: The University of Minnesota Press, 1953), pp. 42, 45, 48 (Study 2).

[6] A similar test-taking attitude on the part of delinquent girls as contrasted with boys has been reported by Capwell; Dora F. Capwell, "Personality Patterns of Adolescent Girls: Delinquents and Nondelinquents," *ibid.*, pp. 29-37 (Study 1).

Table 7. Number of Delinquent and Nondelinquent Students With T-Scores of 70 or Above on Each of the Ten MMPI Clinical Scales

Scale	Boys				Girls				Total (N=234)	
	Delinquent (N=19)		Nondelinquent (N=95)		Delinquent (N=15)		Nondelinquent (N=105)			
	Number	Percent	Number	Percent	Number	Percent	Number	Percent	Number	Percent
1 (Hs)			6	6.3			3	2.9	9	3.8
2 (D)	3	15.8	11	11.6			2	1.9	16	6.8
3 (Hy)							6	5.7	6	2.6
4 (Pd)	10	52.6	11	11.6	9	60.0	22	21.0	52	22.2
5 (Mf)	2	10.5	2	2.1	2	13.3	2	1.9	8	3.4
6 (Pa)	2	10.5	7	7.4	7	46.7	11	10.5	27	11.5
7 (Pt)	2	10.5	16	16.8	2	13.3	8	7.6	28	12.0
8 (Sc)	5	26.3	15	15.8	6	40.0	15	14.3	41	17.5
9 (Ma)	3	15.8	27	28.4	8	53.3	20	19.0	58	24.8
0 (Si)	1	5.3	3	3.2	1	6.7	2	1.9	7	3.0

The MMPI codes of nondelinquent ninth grade students were quite similar to those reported by Hathaway and Monachesi for Minnesota ninth grade boys and girls.[7] The code of the Minnesota boys was 498 7 652301/ FK/L:, that of the girls 4-859 7036/12: FK/L: The similarity of the Kentucky to the Minnesota students is most evident when mean clinical scale scores are compared. Among the girls, the mean difference between the Kentucky and Minnesota subjects was 2.9 T-scores on the 10 scales; among the boys the mean difference was 1.4 T-scores.

The only statistically significant mean scale difference between the Kentucky nondelinquent boys and girls was on scale 2—Depression (t=2.197). The higher D score among boys is, again, similar to Hathaway and Monachesi's findings in Minnesota. The fact that the Kentucky students are, however, somewhat higher on scales 2, 7, and 9 (among the girls, scales 6 and 8 as well) and lower on scale 5 than the Minnesota students seems worthy of note.

Another facet of the analysis of MMPI profiles with regard to differences between delinquents and nondelinquents is presented in Table 6. Employing the commonly accepted T-score of 70 as the cutting point which indicates the likelihood of severe personality aberration, delinquents are contrasted with nondelinquents. Among the delinquents, 90 percent of the boys and 80 percent of the girls have one or more scales 70 or above. Among the nondelinquent boys, 55 percent have at least one T-score 70 or above; the comparable figure for the nondelinquent girls is 43 percent.[8] These data indicate considerably more personality aberration or maladjustment among the delinquents than among the

[7] Starke R. Hathaway and Elio D. Monachesi, "Personality Characteristics of Adolescents as Related to Their Later Careers: Part I. Introduction and General Findings," *ibid.*, pp. 103-104 (Study 6); also, Hathaway, Monachesi and Young, *loc. cit.*, pp. 433-440.

[8] Hathaway and Monachesi report 39 percent of ninth grade boys and 29 percent of the girls having T-scores 70 or above; "Personality Characteristics of Adolescents as Related to their Later Careers: Part II. The Two-Year Follow-Up on Delinquency," *Analyzing and Predicting Juvenile Delinquency with the MMPI*, p. 129 (Study 7).

nondelinquents—as such maladjustment is measured by the MMPI.

A further tabulation of these results, which indicates the percentage of subjects having scores of 70 or above by each of the ten clinical scales, is presented in Table 7. Here it is seen that 52.6 percent of the delinquent boys and 60.0 percent of the delinquent girls have profiles in which the Pd scale is elevated to T-score 70 or higher.[9] From the list of individual codes, it may be seen that 33 of the 34 delinquents have profiles in which the Pd scale is at the T-score 60 level or above. The elevation of scale 8 among the delinquents is also evident. In addition, scales 6 and 9 are markedly elevated among approximately half of the delinquent girls. Table 7 along with the individual codes of the delinquent boys and girls, delineates perhaps even more cogently than the previous analysis the extent of personality deficiency among the incarcerated delinquents.

DISCUSSION

The present findings, when viewed within the context of previous research with the MMPI, seem to warrant several conclusions. The delinquents more than the nondelinquents were found to have maladjusted personalities. As has been consistently reported in previous studies with the MMPI, the delinquent profiles were characterized by the prominence of scale 4, Pd.[10] These findings support the contention that

[9] These results are similar to those obtained in two previous studies. Ashbaugh reports 52 percent of his delinquent sample 70 or above on the Pd scale. James H. Ashbaugh, "Personality Patterns of Juvenile Delinquents in an Area of Small Population," *ibid.*, p. 58 (Study 3). Stanton found that 62 percent of an adult prison population had Pd scores of 69 or above. John M. Stanton, "Group Personality Profile Related to Aspects of Antisocial Behavior," *Journal of Criminal Law, Criminology and Police Science*, Vol. 47 (September-October, 1956), pp. 340-349.

[10] Hathaway and Monachesi, *Analyzing and Predicting Juvenile Delinquency with the MMPI, passim;* A. L. Benton, "The Minnesota Multiphasic Personality Inventory in Clinical Practice," *Journal of Nervous and Mental Disease*, Vol. 102 (July-December, 1945), pp. 416-420; J. C. McKinley and S. R. Hathaway, "The Minnesota

28

delinquents more than nondelinquents have immature, amoral, and rebellious personalities.[11]

In addition to the marked elevation of scale 4 among the delinquents generally, the delinquent girls had significantly higher scores than the nondelinquent girls on scales 6, 8, and 9, suggesting paranoid, schizoid and manic tendencies. These profiles appear to indicate considerably greater personality maladjustment among the delinquent girls than among the delinquent boys. It seems likely that this fact is associated with the sexually promiscuous behavior

---

Multiphasic Personality Inventory: V. Hysteria, Hypomania, and Psychopathic Deviate," *Journal of Applied Psychology*, Vol. 28 (April, 1944), pp. 153-174; Peter P. Rempel, "The Use of Multivariate Statistical Analysis on Minnesota Multiphasic Personality Inventory Scores in the Classification of Delinquent and Nondelinquent High School Boys," *Journal of Consulting Psychology*, Vol. 22 (February, 1958), pp. 17-23; Morris G. Caldwell, "Personality Trends in the Youthful Male Offender," *Journal of Criminal Law, Criminology and Police Science*, Vol. 49 (January-February, 1959), pp. 405-416; James H. Panton, "MMPI Profile Configurations Among Crime Classification Groups," *Journal of Clinical Psychology*, Vol. 14 (July, 1958), pp. 305-308; also Stanton, *loc. cit.*; Robert D. Wirt and Peter F. Briggs, "Personality and Environmental Factors in the Development of Delinquency," *Psychological Monographs*, Vol. 73, No. 15 (1959), pp. 1-47; Sylvan B. Caditz, "Effects of a Forestry Camp Experience on the Personality of Delinquent Boys," *Journal of Clinical Psychology*, Vol. 17 (January, 1961), pp. 78-81; Peter F. Briggs, Robert D. Wirt and Rochelle Johnson, "An Application of Prediction Tables to the Study of Delinquency," *Journal of Consulting Psychology*, Vol. 25 (February, 1961), pp. 46-50; Mary H. Randolph, Harold Richardson and Ronald C. Johnson, "A Comparison of Social and Solitary Male Delinquents," *Journal of Consulting Psychology*, Vol. 25 (August, 1961), pp. 293-295.

[11] The Gluecks in *Unraveling Juvenile Delinquency* delineate a personality structure among delinquent boys which is quite similar to that reported here: impulsiveness, unconventional ideas, extroversiveness, along with suspiciousness. Despite the use of different personality measurement procedures, it is pertinent to note the comparability of findings with respect to the extent of mental pathology in both delinquent and nondelinquent samples. Thus, the Gluecks found "no conspicuous mental pathology" as evidenced in the Rorschach analysis among 48.6 percent of the delinquents and 55.7 percent of the nondelinquents. Sheldon and Eleanor Glueck, *Unraveling Juvenile Delinquency* (Cambridge, Massachusetts: The Commonwealth Fund, 1950), p. 239.

MMPI Codes of Incarcerated Juvenile Delinquents

Delinquent Boys (no.=19)

2'47-89/10 35 6: (27:7:3:17)
4'23 178-650/9: (0:6:4:23)
4'3 81726/590: (0:3:1:21)
43-986 1 72/5:0# (16:4:2:23)
4'72-19 58 0 6/3: (1:4:5:19)
4'8260-795 3/1: (35:6:6:14)
4'83 9-1 75 26/0: (5:4:4:20)
49"3-6 87 5/12:0# (0:1:5:15)
49'827 1/30 56: (1:3:6:20)
5*86'417-30 29/ (0:2:11:7)
8*627"9'4 15 0-3: (0:4:15:10)
8"742'93 5-60 1/ (8:2:8:16)
89 7-5 4 26 3/01: (3:6:13:6)
8"976 4-5 02/1:3# (0:2:10:6)
9'4-5 1638 72/0: (0:2:3:14)
9'4-58 617/23:0# (0:3:2:14)
94'65-78/23 0:1# (0:5:6:10)
95 48'67-012/3: (4:4:13:9)
0'6 47 9-8 5 312/ (0:2:9:8)
Invalids (no.=1)
4'98 267-5310/ (0:3:16:5)

Delinquent Girls (no.=15)

3 94 8-6 15 7/02# (0:3:1:16)
4"6'32 89-7 1 /05: (3:2:11:6)
46'98-23 710/5: (0:3:13:10)
48*9 57 6'2 3-10/ (0:2:14:10)
4*89"67'213-0/5: (0:5:15:13)
49-56/80 1 37:2# (1:2:3:9)
4 96 8-5 7/2 30 1: (0:4:5:10)
4*96'85-73/01 2: (0:2:15:14)
4"9'8-6/31 0 57:2# (4:2:1:14)
4'9 80-72 6/5 3:1# (2:2:8:8)
8*59 46'7-3/1 20: (0:1:10:12)
8"9'14 730-652/ (1:3:12:4)
9'4-68/75 2 03:1# (3:5:7:10)
98"46 0'7-23 15/ (2:2:14:6)
9"8'654-70 1/3:2# (0:4:7:11)
Invalids (no.=3)
48*79"60'2-13/5: (0:4:24:14)
68*4 79"01'2-35/ (0:4:39:4)
84*9"7'36-1/25 0: (0:1:20:17)

and attendant personal disorganization which the female offenders have experienced. The opprobrium which our culture attaches to promiscuous behavior among young girls as well as the deviant motivational forces required to effect such behavior may both be considered as significant factors in this regard.[12]

In addition to the personality maladjustment depicted in the MMPI profiles, the delinquents more than the non-delinquents were failing in the adolescent socialization process. Coming from lower class homes which were frequently

[12] See Ball and Logan, loc. cit.

30

unstable, the delinquents were unable to meet the demands of the educational system. They were usually retarded in grade placement and, apparently, increasingly turning to other pursuits to achieve status, realize excitement, or express hostility. For the boys this commonly involved stealing, for the girls sexual promiscuity.

2

CHARACTERISTICS OF PUBLIC SCHOOL
STUDENTS WITH DELINQUENCY RECORDS

In an effort to assay the extent and character of delinquency in the general population, recent research has been directed toward determining the number of adolescents in various nonincarcerated populations who have committed unlawful acts or who admit to such commissions.[13] To obtain infor-

[13] Various delinquency rates have recently been reported. In a study of 12-year-old boys who were "insulated" against delinquency and those who were delinquency prone, the rates of *police or court contact* varied from 8.3 percent for the insulated boys to 23 percent for the delinquency prone boys; Walter C. Reckless, Simon Dinitz and Barbara Kay, "The Self Component in Potential Delinquency and Potential Non-Delinquency," *American Sociological Review*, Vol. 22 (October, 1957), p. 567. In Nye's study, 32.1 percent of the high school boys aged 16 and 17 *admitted* the commission of illegal acts; F. Ivan Nye, *Family Relationships and Delinquent Behavior* (New York: John Wiley and Sons, 1958), from Table 2.1, p. 16 (the "most delinquent" group, scale types 8-15, constituted 32.1 percent of the total). Hathaway, Monachesi and Young (*loc. cit.*, p. 435) found that 34 percent of a statewide sample of boys had *police or court contact* before age 17.5. Monahan (*loc. cit.*, p. 66) has reported that 22 percent of Philadelphia boys would appear in *court* before age 18. Ball estimates that 30 percent of the boys in a Kentucky metropolitan area would have an official *record* of delinquency before age 18; John C. Ball, "The Extent of Juvenile Delinquency in a Stable Metropolitan Area," *Kentucky Law Journal*, Vol. 49 (Spring, 1961), pp. 363-369. Reiss and Rhodes in their Nashville study found that of *white boys* 16 years of age and over who were *still in school* 8 percent were known to the court as delinquent; Albert J. Reiss, Jr. and Albert Lewis Rhodes, "The Distribution of Juvenile Delinquency in the Social Class Structure," *American Sociological Review*, Vol. 26 (October, 1961), pp. 720-732.

mation on the extent of delinquency among the public school students, police and court records were checked and police and court officials were asked to indicate their knowledge of the commission of specific illegal acts, *whether or not these acts had become part of the official records.*

Of the 234 ninth grade students, 12 boys (11 percent of the boys) were found to have committed delinquent acts. These offenses included larceny (4), auto theft (2), malicious mischief (1), incorrigibility (1), counterfeiting of coins (1), and serious traffic violations (3).

The boys with delinquency records did not differ appreciably from their nondelinquent classmates with respect to age, race, school achievement or retardation, ratings by teachers, after-school employment, family composition or socioeconomic status. But the mean I.Q. of the delinquent boys was 95.0, compared with 104.8 for those without records of deviancy. In addition, these boys were less frequently hometown boys than the nondelinquents (22.2 vs. 60.0 percent), although the small number of cases prompts most cautious interpretations of such differences.

MMPI PROFILES OF BOYS WITH DELINQUENCY RECORDS

Of the 12 public school boys who were known to have committed delinquent acts, nine completed valid MMPI profiles. The MMPI code (9-48 675 3/20 1: F/KL?:) for these nine boys was similar to that of the nondelinquent boys in that Ma was prominent and the "948" pattern evident in both instances. Among these nine delinquent boys, almost half of the codes have scale 9 elevated to the T-score 70 level as well as one or more scales below T-score 40, but the number of subjects is too small to establish a general pattern. Fifty-six percent of the boys with records of delinquency and 55 percent of the boys without such records (N=86) had one or more clinical scales elevated to 70 or above. In view of the overall similarities in the profiles,

32

```
4-3 2581/ 79 60: K-F/?L:
49 86 3-51 7/20: K-L/F?:
5 26 9-743/081: KF L?:
59-32648 07:1# F/LK ?:
8"7 102 4-39 6/5: F-KL?:
8 79'60-54/1:23# F'L?:K#
9'4-5 37 26/80:1# F/LK ?:
9'64 5/0 38:2 17# F/K? :L#
9'7468 3/102:5# F-KL?:
```

we may tentatively conclude that the delinquent boys are
not markedly different from their nondelinquent classmates
with respect to MMPI profiles.

DISCUSSION

The boys with records of delinquency did not differ materi-
ally, then, from their nondelinquent classmates, except in
nativity, intelligence test scores and the prominence of
scale 9 in the MMPI codes. The personality differences are
not marked, although they may be considered as indicative
of some aggressiveness.

3

MINORITY GROUP STATUS
AND PERSONALITY

$\mathcal{T}$*HE STUDY* of personality differences between Negroes and whites in the United States has received considerable attention during the past thirty years, but especially in the past twenty years.[1] Many of these studies have arrived at confusing or conflicting conclusions. As Klineberg observed more than a decade ago, the lack of adequate personality measuring instruments as well as superficial methodology has resulted in inconclusive findings.[2] In addition, it should be added that extraneous value judgments and unfounded opinions have too often been substituted for empirical demonstration.[3] Although delineation of personality differences between groups is quite distinct from a study of etiology, cross-sectional studies would seem to be a prerequisite to, as well as a necessary part of, such etiological research.[4]

In this chapter the Negro and white public school students are compared with respect to their background and their personality profiles. In each of the two towns the Negro and white students attended the same classes and all were enrolled in the ninth grade. The two school systems were integrated in September, 1956, which was the academic year prior to this study.

Although the Negro and white students attended the same schools and lived in the same towns, their ways of life

[1] For example, Gunnar Myrdal, *An American Dilemma* (New York: Harper and Brothers, 1944); Otto Klineberg, ed., *Characteristics of the American Negro* (New York: Harper and Brothers, 1944); Abram Kardiner and Lionel Ovesey, *The Mark of Oppression* (New York: W. W. Norton, 1951); Horace R. Cayton, "The Psychology of the Negro Under Discrimination," *Mental Health and Mental Disorder*, Arnold M. Rose, ed. (New York: W. W. Norton, 1955), chapter 25; Bertram P. Karon, *The Negro Personality* (New York: Springer Publishing Company, 1958).

[2] Klineberg, *op. cit.*, pp. 137-138; on this point see also George Eaton Simpson and J. Milton Yinger, *Racial and Cultural Minorities* (New York: Harper and Brothers, 1958), chapters 6 and 7, especially pp. 224ff.

[3] Myrdal (*op. cit.*) discusses this problem at some length; see Appendix 10, "Quantitative Studies of Race Attitudes." He notes, for example, that "we are not facing a question merely of more or less meager and incorrect knowledge. There is an emotional load of valuation conflicts pressing for rationalization, creating certain blind spots—and also creating a desire for knowledge in other spots—and in general causing conceptions of reality to deviate from truth in determined directions." (p. 1138.)

[4] Klineberg's analysis of previous research pertaining to racial similarities and differences offers some of the most penetrating and comprehensive criticisms. In particular, his observation that it is methodologically impossible to isolate race from cultural context is important for it suggests the definite limitations of the classical experimental model in such research. His emphasis upon the desirability of testing diverse populations under varying conditions is a corollary of the inadequacy of studying only matched groups. See Klineberg, *op. cit.*, Part II, chapters 3-4, especially p. 81; and Part III, chapter 1, especially pp. 112-113.

Table 8. Age, Nativity, Residential Mobility, Intelligence Quotient, School Grades, Educational Retardation, After-School Employment, Family Composition, and Socioeconomic Status of Negro and White Students by Sex[a]

Group	N	Mean Age	Kentucky Nativity, Percent	Local Nativity, Percent	Mean I.Q.	Grade Average	Retarded in school, Percent	Percent Employed Part-Time	Broken Homes, Percent	Lower Class, Percent
Negro Boys	14	15.3	100.0	78.6	96.4	2.9 D**	50.0	42.9	35.7*	85.7*
White Boys	81	15.0	81.3	52.5	104.5	4.7 C	31.2	27.2	8.6	18.5
Negro Girls	17	14.4	94.1	70.6	93.6	4.1 C**	11.8	17.6	29.4	64.7**
White Girls	88	14.8	90.7	62.8	105.3	5.3 C+	18.2	8.0	18.2	15.5

[a] Difference between Negro and white boys, or girls, statistically significant at level of: *P < .05; **P < .01. No test of significance applied to I.Q. data.

were quite distinct. The Negro students lived in a segregated society. With respect to occupation, place of residence, church membership, recreation, and social relations generally, the Negro caste was isolated from the dominant white caste. It is in this sense that the Negroes live in a socially deviant environment.

CHARACTERISTICS OF THE NEGRO SAMPLE

There were 31 Negro students with valid profiles in the ninth grade public school classes to which the MMPI was administered in this study. Of these, 14 were boys and 17 were girls. Of their white classmates, 81 boys and 88 girls also had valid profiles.

The mean age of the 14 Negro boys was 15.3 years, of the 17 Negro girls, 14.4 years. Comparable figures for the 81 white boys and 88 white girls were 15.0 and 14.8 years. The Negro boys, then, were somewhat older than the Negro girls, who in turn were younger than the white students. These age differences were not, however, statistically significant.

The Negro students more often than the whites had been born and brought up in their place of present residence; 79 percent of the Negro boys and 71 percent of the Negro girls were hometown students, compared with 53 percent of the white boys and 63 percent of the girls. Only one Negro student was not a native of Kentucky, while 23 white students were from out of the state (3 percent vs. 14 percent for both sexes).

A record of intelligence test scores was available for only 14 of the 31 Negro students.[5] The mean intelligence quotient for these Negro students was some 8 to 12 points

[5] To what extent this distorts the findings is uncertain. McCary and Tracktir have reported similar differences among Negro and white high school students in Pittsburgh. J. L. McCary and Jack Tracktir, "Relationship Between Intelligence and Frustration-Aggression Patterns as Shown by Two Racial Groups," *Journal of Clinical Psychology*, Vol. 13 (April, 1957), pp. 202-204.

Table 9. Semester Grade Average of Negro and White Public School Students[a]

Semester Grade Average	Boys				Girls			
	Negro		White		Negro		White	
	Number	Percent	Number	Percent	Number	Percent	Number	Percent
8. (A)			4	5.1			3	3.5
7. (B+)	2	14.3	8	10.1	1	5.9	18	20.9
6. (B)			18	22.8	2	11.8	22	25.6
5. (C+)	1	7.1	12	15.2	5	29.4	15	17.4
4. (C)	1	7.1	18	22.8	3	17.6	15	17.4
3. (C-)	2	14.3	10	12.7	3	17.6	9	10.5
2. (D)	4	28.6	7	8.9	2	11.8	4	4.7
1. (D-)	4	28.6	2	2.5	1	5.9		
0. (E)								
Total	14	100.0	79	100.0	17	100.0	86	100.0
Mean Grade	2.93		4.73		4.12		5.26	

a Four white students, two male and two female, were omitted from the table as no grades were available.

Significance of difference in grades between Negro and white students: Boys t = 3.47, P < .001; Girls t = 2.76, P < .01.

lower than that for the whites (see Table 8). The limitations of the I.Q. data referred to in the previous chapter apply to this comparison.

The Negro boys were retarded more in grade placement and the Negro girls less than either of the white groups. Among Negro boys, 50 percent were retarded one or more years. For both Negroes and whites, boys were retarded more than girls. Comparable differences are found with regard to school achievement. The Negro boys received the lowest grades of the four groups of students. Considering the percentage of academic failures—those averaging D or below—even more marked differences are evident, for 57 percent of the Negro boys were in this category compared with only 18 percent of the Negro girls, 11 percent of the white boys, and 5 percent of the white girls. The Negro boys, then, are markedly lower than the Negro girls and white students of both sexes with respect to academic achievement.

Both Negro boys and girls were employed during after-school hours more often than white students. The percentages of Negro boys, Negro girls, white boys and white girls who held such jobs were 42.9, 17.6, 27.2 and 8.0. Of those who were employed, the mean hours worked were quite similar for the four groups of students: 16.5, 12.5, 13.3 and 13.2, for the Negro boys and girls and white boys and girls respectively.

Both Negro and white boys most commonly held delivery or helper jobs. The latter kind of employment was more frequent among Negroes (50.0 percent vs. 14.3 percent) while delivery jobs, especially paper routes, were more frequent among the white boys (76.2 percent vs. 33.3 percent). The Negro and white girls worked after school mainly as clerks and babysitters; no differences between the two groups were evident in this regard.

Negro students more frequently than the whites came from broken homes. The percentage of Negro boys, Negro girls, white boys and white girls whose home life was broken

Table 10. Socioeconomic Status of Negro and White Ninth Grade Students as Ranked on the Minnesota Scale for Paternal Occupations

Class	Socio-economic Status	Boys				Girls*			
		Negro		White		Negro		White	
		Number	Percent	Number	Percent	Number	Percent	Number	Percent
Upper	1			8	9.9			7	8.3
	2			12	14.8			12	14.3
Middle	3	1	7.1	19	23.5	3	17.6	21	25.0
	4			1	1.2	1	5.9	3	3.6
	5	1	7.1	26	32.1	2	11.8	28	33.3
Lower	6	9	64.3	5	6.2	9	52.9	10	11.9
	7	3	21.4	10	12.3	2	11.8	3	3.6
	Total	14	100.0	81	100.0	17	100.0	84	100.0

* Four cases omitted

Difference in socioeconomic status between Negro and white students: Boys $X^2 = 26.60$, $P < .001$; Girls $X^2 = 20.01$, $P < .001$.

by divorce, separation or death was, respectively, 35.7, 29.4, 8.6 and 18.2.[6]

Clearly, the Negro students are predominantly from families of lower socioeconomic status. Some 86 percent of the Negro boys and 65 percent of the Negro girls are from the two lowest classes; by contrast, only 19 percent of the white boys and 16 percent of the girls are from similar socioeconomic strata.

MMPI PROFILES: NEGRO AND WHITE

The Negro boys had significantly higher mean scores than the white boys on only one MMPI scale, Hs. In addition, the Negro boys were higher on the Depression Scale and the F scale, although both of these differences were below the .05 percent significance level.

The Negro girls were significantly higher than the white girls on the Sc and Si scales as well as on the F scale; they were lower than the whites on the Hy and K scales. There are, then, more marked personality differences between the Negro girls and white girls than is the case with the boys.

Within the Negro group, the boys had a significantly higher mean score on the K scale and a lower score on the Si scale than the girls ($P < .05$). Among the white students, the girls were significantly higher on the L and K scales. These mean scores—but not the t values—are presented in Table 11.

The MMPI codes of the Negro and white ninth grade students were as follows:

	Boys	Girls
Negro	9 847-21 6503/ F/LK ?:	849-067 52/13: F-LK?:
White	9-487 60523 1/ F/KL ?:	49-8763 052/1: FKL/?:

[6] Deutsch found that 55 percent of Negro school children in a metropolitan area came from broken homes while only 9 percent of the white control group came from such homes. Martin Deutsch, "Minority Group and Class Status as Related to Social and Personality Factors in Scholastic Achievement," *Society for Applied Anthropology*, Monograph No. 2, 1960, p. 8.

41

Table 11. MMPI Mean Scale Scores, Standard Deviations, and t Values of Negro and White Public School Students[a]

Scale	Boys					Girls				
	Negro N=14		White N=81		t-Test	Negro N=17		White N=88		t-Test
	Mean	S.D.	Mean	S.D.		Mean	S.D.	Mean	S.D.	
?	3.5	4.17	7.3	11.71	1.187	4.0	6.36	2.9	8.58	0.493
L	4.4	1.80	3.4	2.06	1.669	3.3	1.71	4.2	2.06	1.611
F	7.4	3.08	5.7	3.40	1.658	8.8	2.69	5.2	3.28	4.127**
K	12.6	5.30	11.8	4.37	0.627	9.1	2.63	13.7	4.76	3.851**
1 (Hs)	56.4	12.36	50.4	8.67	2.195*	49.4	7.14	49.5	8.69	0.055
2 (D)	58.1	12.35	53.3	11.22	1.441	52.2	6.51	50.6	8.53	0.731
3 (Hy)	52.6	6.88	52.8	6.61	0.082	47.3	7.47	53.8	8.88	2.819**
4 (Pd)	60.9	9.45	59.5	9.02	0.540	61.2	10.51	61.0	10.26	0.052
5 (Mf)	53.7	7.43	53.5	8.09	0.084	53.5	8.01	51.2	8.62	0.994
6 (Pa)	54.1	8.79	54.3	8.77	0.050	57.8	9.51	55.7	9.67	0.822
7 (Pt)	60.1	7.30	58.0	10.68	0.678	57.5	6.69	57.2	8.78	0.117
8 (Sc)	61.4	10.55	59.0	10.13	0.807	66.2	8.64	58.6	9.19	3.126**
9 (Ma)	63.3	9.58	62.1	11.22	0.373	60.1	5.81	60.4	10.20	0.149
0 (Si)	53.4	8.66	53.6	8.97	0.081	58.4	6.30	51.7	7.90	3.254**

[a] Validity scales are reported in mean raw scores, clinical scales in mean T-scores. K corrections have been applied to scales 1, 4, 7, 8, and 9. Significance of difference between means: *P < .05; **P < .01.

These group codes and the accompanying list of individual codes for the Negro students indicate certain personality differences between the Negroes and whites. The Negro profiles, in the first place, are elevated to a greater extent than the white profiles. There are four scales elevated to the T-score 60 level among the Negro boys and three scales so elevated among the Negro girls; these elevated scales contrast with one such elevation in the code of the white boys and two among the white girls. This mean elevation is not the result of a disproportionate number of Negro profiles above the T-score 70 level. The elevation of the Negro profiles is found in the T-score 60 to 70 range.

With respect to profile configuration, the most marked features of the Negro boys' code were neurotic tendencies, over-sensitivity, and the decreased prominence of Pd. The prominence of scales 8 and 7 in the T-score 60-70 range and scale 2 in fifth code position should be noted. Further, from the list of individual codes (as well as from Table 12) it may be observed that scale 1, 2, or 7 is in first position in half of the Negro boys' codes. The elevation of scale 2, Depression, is especially noticeable in the individual codes, while the prominence of 7 is most evident in the group code. The Negro boys have fewer codes beginning with Pd than the white boys. In this respect, the group code is misleading since it does not indicate the greater frequency of codes beginning with Pd among the white boys (see Table 12). The contrast with regard to the Pd scale is even more striking between the Negroes and delinquents; 42 percent of the latter group have codes in which scale 4 is in first position (see Figure 1).

The Negro girls are characterized by introversion and prominence of schizoid tendencies in their MMPI codes. Scale 0 or 8 is first in code position for more than half of the girls; in three additional cases 8 is second in order. Indeed, in 14 of the 17 codes, Sc is elevated to a T-score of 60 or more—in five of these it is 70 or above. Correspondingly, there are fewer codes beginning with Ma than among

Table 12. First Scale in MMPI Code of Delinquent and Nondelinquent Students by Race and Sex

First Scale in Code	Boys						Girls						Total (N=234) Percent
	Delinquent		Nondelinquent White		Nondelinquent Negro		Delinquent		Nondelinquent White		Nondelinquent Negro		
	N	Pct.	N	Pct.	N	Pct.	N	Pct.	N	Pct.	N	Pct.	
1. (Hs)			2	2.5	2	14.3							1.7
2. (D)	1	5.3	9	11.1	4	28.6			2	2.3			6.8
3. (Hy)			2	2.5			1	6.7	5	5.7			3.4
4. (Pd)	8	42.1	12	14.8	1	7.1	9	60.0	22	25.0	3	17.6	23.5
5. (Mf)	1	5.3	5	6.2					5	5.7			4.7
6. (Pa)			2	2.5					5	5.7	1	5.9	3.4
7. (Pt)			6	7.4	1	7.1			9	10.2	1	5.9	7.3
8. (Sc)	4	21.1	9	11.1	1	7.1	2	13.3	9	10.2	6	35.3	13.2
9. (Ma)	4	21.1	27	33.3	5	35.7	3	20.0	25	28.4	2	11.8	28.2
0. (Si)	1	5.3	7	8.6					6	6.8	4	23.5	7.7
Total	19	100.0	81	100.0	14	100.0	15	100.0	88	100.0	17	100.0	100.0

white girls. This lessening of adolescent energy appears to be associated with the introversion and sensitivity suggested by the prominence of scales 0 and 8. The prominence of these personality patterns is also evident when the Negro and white students are grouped into four scale types according to highest MMPI scale.[7]

With regard to the validity scales, it seems probable that the low K scores combined with low L scores and high F scores portray unusual frankness on the part of the Negro girls. The higher F scores among both the Negro boys and girls would appear to reflect personality maladjustment to some extent.

DISCUSSION

With respect to both background characteristics and personality variables, significant differences were found between Negro and white ninth grade students. In general, the greater educational retardation, poor scholastic achievement, lower intelligence quotients, prevalence of broken homes and lower class status among the Negro subjects is similar to the delineation provided by previous studies.[8] The fact that the greater part of the Negro population is confined to a segregated lower socioeconomic stratum is significant in that this cultural context is undoubtedly associated with the other evidences of deviancy or failure in the middle class socialization process.

Beyond the more apparent facts of the place Negroes occupy in contemporary American society, several points

[7] John C. Ball, "Comparison of MMPI Profile Differences Among Negro-White Adolescents," *Journal of Clinical Psychology*, Vol. 16 (July, 1960), pp. 304-307.

[8] For an extended discussion of the relationship of social factors to intellectual and personality differences among various racial and cultural population see Kardiner and Ovesey, *op. cit.*, Parts II and III. For a recent study in which the differential class composition of the Negro and white populations (when the same criteria are employed in ascertaining social class) is documented, see August B. Hollingshead and Frederick C. Redlich, *Social Class and Mental Illness: A Community Study* (New York: John Wiley and Sons, 1958), p. 202.

Figure 1. Percentage of Delinquent, White, and Negro Students with Various First Scales in MMPI Code

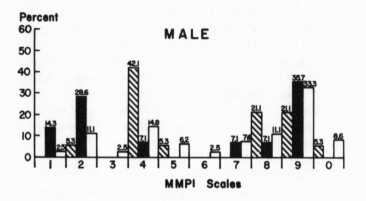

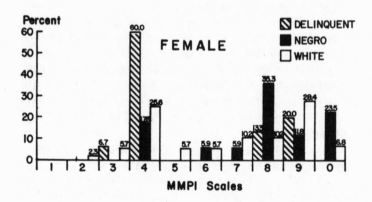

Source: Text, Table 12.

46

stand out with reference to the Negro students included in this study. Since the two public school systems were integrated the previous year without disturbance, the Negro and white students had been attending classes together for almost two academic years. Comparisons of grade averages, for example, are therefore meaningful. The prior elementary school education of the two groups, however, was not similar. The extent to which earlier segregated schooling affected present academic achievement, or affected the developmnt of personality, is unknown. All that can reasonably be stated are the present similarities and differences that exist between the two groups.

The Negro girls are faring considerably better than the boys in school; they are not far below the white boys in academic achievement. Indeed, the Negro girls are retarded less in grade placement than either of the white groups. The Negro boys, on the other hand, are clearly failing to obtain satisfactory grades, and are the most retarded of the four groups. It seems likely that this rather marked sex difference in socialization reflects the divergent expectations among lower class adolescents. The Negro boys are going to compete economically in a society governed by middle class norms; they have already, perhaps, recognized that they will be competing disadvantageously. The Negro girls have more interest in establishing a family and have occupational expectations which are less competitive. Whether or not the Negro girls do as mothers assume a major economic responsibility in the future is another question.[9]

Deutsch's study of Negro children in a "racially encapsulated area" of a northern metropolitan slum presents data which are strikingly similar to the present findings. He found the Negro children to be faring less successfully in school than the whites, and the Negro boys to be doing

[9] Frazier describes the American Negro family as influenced by a semi-matriarchal structure. It seems likely that this family pattern may be related to personality differences between Negro boys and girls. E. Franklin Frazier, *The Negro Family in the United States* (New York: The Dryden Press, 1948), chapter 7.

47

significantly more poorly than the girls. In this regard, Deutsch observes that the Negro girl is less in conflict with middle-class values, while "the Negro boy receives the brunt of the negative implications of his situation."[10]

Previous studies of personality differences between Negroes and whites have usually stressed the pervasiveness of aggressive tendencies within the Negro population. Goldfarb reports that, "Another universal trait in this group is a sweeping, pushing, impelling hostility or aggressive inclination."[11] More recently, Karon found that Negroes had pronounced difficulties in handling aggressive feelings and fears.[12] In addition to internalized aggressiveness, neurotic tendencies have been reported. On this point, Goldfarb states, "Profound anxiety is hypothesized in all the records."[13]

Comparison of the present MMPI findings with previous personality research is complicated by two considerations. First, the use of diverse measurement procedures precludes the possibility of statistical comparisons. Second, the selection of diverse samples as to age, sex, education, class, and region (while necessary in order to expand our knowledge of the distribution of variables within the entire Negro population) complicates the problem of ascertaining the relative validity of specific personality differences. This latter consideration is especially restrictive in view of the meager personality data extant.[14]

[10] Deutsch, *op. cit.*, p. 12.
[11] William Goldfarb, "The Rorschach Experiment," in Kardiner and Ovesey, *op. cit.*, p. 325.
[12] Karon, *op. cit.*, chapters 6-10.
[13] Goldfarb, *loc. cit.*
[14] Stanton compared 100 Negro and 100 white Sing Sing inmates and found no significant differences on the MMPI scales between the two groups. John M. Stanton, "Group Personality Profile Related to Aspects of Antisocial Behavior," *Journal of Criminal Law, Criminology and Police Science*, Vol. 47 (September-October, 1956), pp. 340-349. Hokanson and Calden compared Negro and white hospital patients on the MMPI. They found the Negroes higher on the Mf, Sc and Ma scales, lower on the Pd scale. Significantly, the highest scale among the Negro patients was Sc, while the whites peaked on the Pd scale.

The present MMPI findings do not reveal the presence of more pronounced aggressive tendencies among the Negro students than among the white students. Indeed, the individual codes reveal less aggressiveness on the part of the Negroes. Scales 4 and 9 are less prominent in the Negro codes. Pertinent, too, is the fact that paranoid tendencies are not present among the Negro adolescents.

MMPI Codes of Ninth Grade Negro Students

Boys (N=14)	Girls (N=17)
12'3458 9-76/0: (0:8:2:23)	4'18 2-70 39 56/ (0:2:10:11)
1 20-59 3/76 84: (4:3:7:8)	48'69 31-702/5# (4:3:9:9)
2'1478 3-96/05: (9:6:7:16)	4'9-25 80/7 136: (15:5:6:7)
21'08 47-36/59: (3:2:8:7)	6'98 4-513/720: (1:1:7:7)
2 781'49 35-6/0: (2:7:6:19)	7 86 9-24 50/13: (0:3:13:8)
287 45-60 9/13: (1:3:11:9)	84'609-721/35: (1:3:13:10)
48"69'7 10-3/25: (5:5:12:13)	8-579 34/10 2:6# (7:3:3:15)
79'0 28-54/63:1# (1:4:7:4)	8"645 0-27/91:3# (2:2:11:9)
84-9 37 5/1 62 0: (0:3:4:16)	8'647902-5/13: (2:7:11:9)
94-758/032:16# (2:6:4:12)	8"7 69'45 0-2/13: (1:0:11:10)
95-4 267/03 18: (1:4:5:8)	80-6 4793 25/1: (1:3:6:14)
9"6'481-735/02: (16:5:10:20)	9 4-6 0 387/521: (0:6:10:5)
9 68 7 0-15 42/3: (4:2:13:11)	9 87-605/124:3# (2:3:9:5)
9'7468 3/102:5# (1:3:7:11)	04-9 278 6/35:1# (0:2:5:8)
	05789-13/46 2: (25:5:9:11)
	05 8-679/421 3: (2:4:7:7)
	08 17-95 46 2/3: (5:4:9:10)

Their findings, then, indicate similar personality differences between Negro and white adults to those reported here among adolescents, except that their subjects were hospital patients and notably more neurotic than the public school students. Jack E. Hokanson and George Calden, "Negro-White Differences on the MMPI," *Journal of Clinical Psychology*, Vol. 16 (January, 1960), pp. 32-33. Miller, Wertz and Counts found their Negro subjects to be higher on the L, Hs and Ma scales and lower on the Mf scale than whites. Christine Miller, Clara Wertz and Sarah Counts, "Racial Differences on the MMPI," *Journal of Clinical Psychology*, Vol. 17 (April, 1961), pp. 159-161.

The Negro profiles are characterized by neurotic tendencies, sensitivity, and introversion. The Negro boys are more neurotic than the girls; they are unduly concerned with bodily health and are more depressed. The Negro girls are markedly introverted and sensitive in personal relations. There is evidence of a lack of social sophistication and an absence of adolescent energy on the part of these girls. In sum, the Negro students were found to be more withdrawn and neurotic than the white students.

4

SOCIAL CLASS AND
ADOLESCENT PERSONALITY

𝒯HE PERVASIVE influence of class membership in American society has been extensively documented. For instance, we know that children from lower class homes have only a remote chance of entering or graduating from college.[1] We know that the fathers of National Merit scholars come predominantly from certain occupational groups.[2] We know that increasingly both managerial and professional positions are being filled by college graduates.[3] And we know that there is a preponderance of social and personality maladjustment in the lower classes.[4] In view of these facts the question arises as to the effect of different class membership upon the personality and behavior patterns of adolescents.

It may be maintained that lower class behavior and values are themselves deviant in middle class American society. Not only are numerous socially disapproved forms of deviancy associated with low socioeconomic status, but low status itself is commonly regarded as prima facie evidence of failure or deviancy. Conversely, high socioeconomic status is taken as public proof of success. Thus, one's class position has manifest implications with regard to personality and behavior.

In this chapter the public school students with valid MMPI profiles are analyzed with respect to social class differences in background and personality. The subjects were divided into several ranks or classes by means of the Minnesota Scale for Paternal Occupations (also known as the Goodenough-Anderson Scale). On this scale the highest socioeconomic class is ranked one, the lowest seven. While it is advisable to bear in mind that this classification can best be thought of as a continuum with respect to socioeconomic status rather than as indicating social class in a strictly ideological sense, it seems convenient to refer to the three-fold combination of scale ranks as upper, middle and lower class.[5] Ranks 1-2 are designated upper class, 3-5 middle

[1] Raymond A. Mulligan, "Socio-Economic Background and College Enrollment," *American Sociological Review*, Vol. 16 (April, 1951), pp. 188-196.

[2] Horace Mann Bond, "The Productivity of National Merit Scholars by Occupational Class," *School and Society*, Vol. 85 (September 28, 1957), pp. 267-268.

[3] William H. Whyte, Jr., *The Organization Man* (New York: Doubleday, 1957), chapter 9, "The Pipe Line."

[4] August B. Hollingshead and Frederick C. Redlich, *Social Class and Mental Illness: A Community Study* (New York: John Wiley and Sons, 1958); Bradley Buell and Associates, *Community Planning for Human Services* (New York: Columbia University Press, 1952).

[5] The present classification by parental occupation yields results which are quite similar to those obtained by means of social class indexes. Hollingshead reports a correlation of .881 between occupation and judged class position (Hollingshead and Redlich, *op. cit.*, p. 394); for a further discussion see Joseph A. Kahl and J. A. Davis, "A Comparison of Indexes of Socio-Economic Status," *American Sociological Review*, Vol. 20 (June, 1955), pp. 317-325.

class, and 6-7 lower class. Class 1 includes professional persons, class 2 semiprofessional and managerial, class 3 skilled trades and retail businesses, class 4 farmers, class 5 semiskilled occupations, minor clerical positions and minor businesses, class 6 slightly skilled trades and other occupations requiring little training, and class 7 laborers.

CHARACTERISTICS OF THE THREE CLASSES

A *rating* of socioeconomic status was obtained for 196 of the 200 ninth grade students with valid MMPI profiles. Of this group, 19.9 percent were rated as upper class, 54.1 percent as middle class and 26.0 percent as lower class. The mean ages of the six groups were quite similar (Table 13). The only notable age difference was with respect to lower class boys, who were six months older than middle class boys.

There was a positive relationship between mobility and socioeconomic status. The higher status adolescents were less often of Kentucky nativity and less likely to have been born in the town of present residence. This trend is most evident with respect to the upper class students, among whom 60 percent were not native to their town of school attendance.[6]

Intelligence test scores were higher among the upper socioeconomic groups than the lower. The mean I.Q. of both the upper class boys and girls was 109. The lowest mean I.Q. was that of the lower class girls—95.[7]

[6] This incidence of mobility is greater than that reported in an earlier study by Hollingshead. He found that 81 percent of the young people were local residents since birth. August B. Hollingshead, *Elmtown's Youth* (New York: John Wiley and Sons, 1949), p. 14.

[7] The association of higher intelligence test scores with higher socioeconomic status has consistently been reported. On this point Kenneth Eells states: "All these studies are virtually unanimous in finding that children from 'high' or 'favorable' socioeconomic backgrounds tend to secure higher scores on the usual intelligence tests (both individual and group) than do children from lower or less favorable socioeconomic backgrounds." Kenneth Eells, *et al., Intelligence and Cultural Differences* (Chicago: The University of Chicago Press, 1951), p. 4.

Table 13. Age, Nativity, Residential Mobility, Intelligence Quotient, School Grades, Educational Retardation, After-School Employment, and Family Composition of Upper, Middle, and Lower Class Students by Sex[a]

Group	N	Mean Age	Kentucky Nativity Percent	Local Nativity Percent	Mean I.Q.	Grade Average	Retarded in school Percent	Percent Employed Part-Time	Broken Homes Percent
Upper Class Boys	20	14.8	75.0	30.0*	109.4	5.6 B-**	15.0**	40.0	0.0
Middle Class Boys	48	14.9	83.0	59.6*	102.4	4.5 C*	27.3**	22.9	14.6
Lower Class Boys	27	15.4*	92.6	70.4*	99.7	3.6 C-*	59.3**	33.3	18.5
Upper Class Girls	19	14.8	78.9	47.4	109.1	5.8 B-**	5.3**	5.3	5.3*
Middle Class Girls	58	14.7	94.7	64.9	105.4	5.2 C+*	12.1**	8.6	15.5*
Lower Class Girls	24	14.9	91.3	69.6	95.0	4.4 C*	41.7**	16.7	37.5*

[a] Differences among boys, or girls, were statistically significant at level of: *P < .05; **P < 01. No test of significance applied to I.Q. data.

Academic achievement was clearly related to socio-economic status. The higher status students were more likely to be receiving superior grades in school and less likely to be failing. Thus, 61 percent of the upper class students received a grade of B or above, compared with only 26 percent of the lower class! In addition, 28 percent of the lower class students were failing (a grade of D or less) compared with 5 percent in the upper class (Table 14). The grade variation by class was more marked among the boys than among the girls. Further, the sex differences in grades decreased as socioeconomic status increased—the upper class boys were doing almost as well as the upper class girls.

Educational retardation was similarly related to class. The higher status students were less frequently retarded in grade placement for their age than those of lower status. These differences are statistically significant and of considerable magnitude. Thus, lower class boys and girls are more than four times as frequently retarded as upper class students. Indeed, 59 percent of the lower class boys and 42 percent of the lower class girls are retarded in their grade placement (Table 13).

Part-time employment after school was not related to class differences, although such employment was more common among boys than girls. Of the boys who worked, the type of employment was quite similar in the lower and middle classes—delivery work, attendants or helpers, and work at home. All of the upper class boys who worked after school held delivery jobs; most of these were paper routes.[8]

Boys and girls of lower socioeconomic status are more likely to be from homes broken by divorce, separation, or death than those of higher status. Only among the girls, however, were the reported differences statistically significant,

[8] There is reason to believe on the basis of these data that part-time employment is not a handicap to the adolescent attending high school. Indeed, Youman's findings indicate that it may be a positive factor—at least, in rural areas—in furthering achievement orientation. E. Grant Youmans, "Factors in Educational Attainment," *Rural Sociology*, Vol. 24 (March, 1959), pp. 21-28.

Table 14. Semester Grade Average of Upper, Middle, and Lower Class Students[a]

Semester Grade Average	Upper Class			Middle Class			Lower Class		
	Number		Total, Percent	Number		Total, Percent	Number		Total, Percent
	Boys	Girls		Boys	Girls		Boys	Girls	
8. (A)	3	2	13.2	1	1	1.9			
7. (B+)	2	4	15.8	4	10	13.5	4	4	16.0
6. (B)	6	6	31.6	9	16	24.0	3	2	10.0
5. (C+)	3	4	18.4	8	11	18.3	2	4	12.0
4. (C)	3	2	13.2	13	10	22.1	3	5	16.0
3. (C−)	1		2.6	7	7	13.5	4	5	18.0
2. (D)	1	1	5.3	3	2	4.8	7	2	18.0
1. (D−)				2		1.9	4	1	10.0
0. (E)									
Total	19	19	100.0	47	57	1u0.0	27	23	100.0
Mean Grade	5.58	5.79		4.49	5.16		3.63	4.35	

* Four cases omitted; two boys and two girls

Significance of Grade Difference by Class:

	Upper-Middle	Upper-Lower	Middle-Lower
Boys	P < .02	P < .01	P < .10
Girls	P < .20	P < .01	P < .05

with 5 percent of the upper class, 15 percent of the middle class and 37 percent of the lower class girls from broken homes (Table 13).

CLASS DIFFERENCES IN MMPI PROFILES

In Table 15 the mean MMPI scale scores of the upper, middle, and lower class boys are presented. Significant mean differences were obtained on the F and Ma scales. The lower class boys were higher than either the middle or upper class groups on the F scale. On the Ma scale, the upper class boys were higher than the middle class boys.

The mean MMPI scores of the upper, middle, and lower class girls were significantly different on scales F, K and Si. The lower class girls were higher on F and lower on K than the upper class girls. On the Si scale, the lower class girls were higher than either of the other groups.

The MMPI codes of the three classes were:

	Boys	Girls
Upper Class	97-48 65 302/1: F/KL ?:	84796 35/10 2: KF/L?:
Middle Class	9-48 7 20536 1/ F/KL?:	94 8 76 30 25/1: F LK/?:
Lower Class	948-7 6 20135/ F-L/K?:	48-9 706 253/1: F-L/K?:

These codes delineate quite different personality configurations in the three classes. Among the boys, the upper class has a code in which Pt is prominent along with Ma, a fact which suggests a certain compulsiveness and rigidity as well as energetic tendencies. It may be noted that the energy component is less closely associated with the unconventionality of Pd than in the middle and lower classes. In the middle class boys' code, Ma is dominant and D is comparatively high. This configuration appears to denote an energetic and slightly dissatisfied personality profile. The lower class code is characterized by the prominence of Pd and Sc, in addition to Ma. This combination suggests unsociable or deviant tendencies in conjunction with a with-

57

Table 15. MMPI Mean Scale Scores, Standard Deviations, and t Values of Upper, Middle, and Lower Class Boys[a]

Scale	Upper Class N=20		Middle Class N=46		Lower Class N=27		t-Test Upper-Middle	t-Test Upper-Lower	t-Test Middle-Lower
	Mean	S.D.	Mean	S.D.	Mean	S.D.			
?	10.1	18.14	5.3	7.28	6.9	8.76	1.543	0.794	0.827
L	3.3	2.17	3.4	2.02	4.0	1.95	0.224	1.156	1.209
F	5.3	3.47	5.4	3.23	7.5	3.19	0.107	2.186*	2.659*
K	11.5	4.14	12.3	4.44	11.7	4.90	0.680	0.210	0.453
1 (Hs)	49.3	9.21	51.0	8.40	53.1	11.20	0.737	1.227	0.918
2 (D)	51.6	8.52	55.1	11.60	53.8	12.94	1.196	0.641	0.443
3 (Hy)	52.1	8.21	53.4	5.95	52.3	6.44	0.733	0.096	0.746
4 (Pd)	59.4	10.08	58.9	7.51	61.5	10.54	0.220	0.683	1.235
5 (Mf)	55.7	6.99	53.5	7.96	52.0	8.39	1.060	1.553	0.739
6 (Pa)	56.0	9.17	53.0	8.14	55.2	9.21	1.292	0.263	1.067
7 (Pt)	60.3	12.66	56.7	8.99	59.8	9.98	1.302	0.155	1.345
8 (Sc)	58.7	10.96	58.8	9.94	60.7	10.04	0.018	0.648	0.819
9 (Ma)	67.3	11.82	60.1	9.47	62.3	11.67	2.573*	1.390	0.870
0 (Si)	52.0	6.58	54.1	9.49	53.7	9.25	0.922	0.693	0.200

[a] Validity scales are reported in mean raw scores, clinical scales in mean T-scores. K corrections have been applied to scales 1, 4, 7, 8, and 9. Significance of difference between means: *P < .05; **P < .01.

drawal from, or perhaps a failure successfully to enter, conventional social activities.

A marked contrast between the code of the upper class girls and those of the middle and lower classes is notable. Besides the obvious absence of scores above 60, there are low scores on Hs, D, and Si. The upper class girls, then, are characterized by an absence of personality maladjustment. Among the middle class girls, there is the prominence of Ma and Pd. This would appear to delineate a personality pattern similar to that of the middle class boys, except that mild depression tendencies are less evident. In the code of the lower class girls, Sc is prominent along with Pd, while Si is higher. This pattern suggests withdrawal and unsociability, combined with the more common adolescent energy and unconventionality indicated by Ma and Pd.

The inverse relationship of psychopathic and neurotic elevations with socioeconomic status among both boys and girls seems worthy of note. This relationship obtains with respect to the F and Pd scales. Both lower class groups (boys and girls) have codes in which Pd is dominant and the F scale elevated. Conversely, among the girls the K scale is associated with high status.

DISCUSSION

Previous studies have either directly or indirectly provided information pertaining to the effect of class or status upon personality as portrayed by the MMPI. Gough's study of high and low status senior high school students offers tentative support to the finding of more elevated profiles in the lower classes, although his combining of males and females excludes the possibility of meaningful comparisons with the present findings.[9] The failure to find significant class differences in MMPI mean scores may be attributed, at least in part, to the increased selectivity of the sample;

[9] Harrison G. Gough, "A New Dimension of Status: I. Development of a Personality Scale," *American Sociological Review*, Vol. 13 (August, 1948), pp. 401-409.

Table 16. MMPI Mean Scale Scores, Standard Deviations, and t Values of Upper, Middle, and Lower Class Girls[a]

Scale	Upper Class N=19		Middle Class N=58		Lower Class N=24		t-Test Upper-Middle	t-Test Upper-Lower	t-Test Middle-Lower
	Mean	S.D.	Mean	S.D.	Mean	S.D.			
?	3.4	4.37	3.0	10.10	2.9	5.61	0.167	0.314	0.045
L	3.3	1.58	4.0	2.00	4.3	2.03	1.475	1.702	0.471
F	4.5	3.88	5.8	3.07	7.3	3.55	1.519	2.420*	1.875
K	15.3	5.12	12.9	4.52	10.9	4.48	1.878	2.896**	1.804
1 (Hs)	49.7	4.98	49.7	9.60	49.3	7.88	0.013	0.190	0.166
2 (D)	48.4	8.89	51.0	8.10	53.3	7.34	1.176	1.938	1.187
3 (Hy)	54.3	6.26	53.5	9.23	50.5	10.10	0.346	1.405	1.290
4 (Pd)	58.2	8.59	60.9	10.77	63.7	10.20	0.995	1.854	1.080
5 (Mf)	50.9	7.04	50.9	8.38	52.2	8.14	0.039	0.505	0.639
6 (Pa)	56.2	10.68	56.5	9.24	56.3	9.39	0.133	0.029	0.110
7 (Pt)	57.8	10.68	57.1	8.60	57.3	6.09	0.266	0.188	0.079
8 (Sc)	59.9	11.81	59.1	9.22	62.6	7.88	0.317	0.871	1.623
9 (Ma)	56.8	8.08	61.9	10.41	59.3	7.64	1.915	1.032	1.063
0 (Si)	49.5	8.77	52.5	7.10	57.1	7.94	1.488	2.889**	2.517*

[a] Validity scales are reported in mean raw scores, clinical scales in mean T-scores. K corrections have been applied to scales 1, 4, 7, 8, and 9. Significance of differences between means: *$P < .05$; **$P < .01$.

Gough's subjects were high school *seniors*. The selectiveness of the educational system with respect to socioeconomic status has the effect of producing a more and more homogeneous school population. This selective factor undoubtedly accounts for the similarity of personality profiles among both male and female college students reported by Black and Goodstein.[10]

Hathaway and Monachesi's comparison of ninth grade children from high rent blocks with those from low rent blocks offers findings which are more clearly related to the present data. They indicate dominance of scales 2 and 4 among the low rent children and greater prominence of 3, 5, and 9 among the high rent children.[11] Again, differences in presentation and design make detailed comparison impossible, but there appears to be general agreement as to class differences in personality. In both the Minnesota and Kentucky studies the prominence of antisocial and general maladjustive tendencies (Pd and D) among low status boys was noted, as well as greater dominance of energetic or optimistic tendencies (Ma) among high status boys.[12] The high Ma scores among upper class boys seem especially worthy of

[10] J. D. Black, "MMPI Results for Fifteen Groups of Female College Students," *Basic Readings on the MMPI in Psychology and Medicine*, George Welsh and W. Grant Dahlstrom, eds. (Minneapolis: University of Minnesota Press, 1956), pp. 562-573; Leonard D. Goodstein, "Regional Differences in MMPI Responses Among Male College Students," *Journal of Consulting Psychology*, Vol. 18 (December, 1954), pp. 437-441.

[11] Starke R. Hathaway and Elio D. Monachesi, "Personality Characteristics of Adolescents as Related to Their Later Careers: Part I. Introduction and General Findings," *Analyzing and Predicting Juvenile Delinquency With the MMPI*, Hathaway and Monachesi, eds. (Minneapolis: The University of Minnesota Press, 1953), pp. 105-106 (Study 6).

[12] In a separate comparison of class differences with delinquent-nondelinquent differences on the MMPI among the boys of this study, Turk found that Ma scores were associated with class differences while high Pd scores were associated with delinquency. Austin T. Turk, "Comparative Performance of Delinquent and Nondelinquent Boys on the MMPI" (unpublished Master's Thesis, Department of Sociology, University of Kentucky, 1959).

note. In general, such scores among nonpatient groups have been interpreted as indicative of over-activity, elation, or optimism.[13] The low status girls in both instances were characterized by antisocial tendencies and interpersonal sensitivity (Pd and Sc) to a greater extent than high status girls.

The contention that high K scores are associated with high socioeconomic status is supported by the Kentucky data only with respect to the girls.[14] The inverse relationship of high status to elevation of the F scale is, however, corroborated; this tendency is particularly evident in the lower class profiles. The previously reported association of high Mf scores for boys with high status is also in accord with the present findings.[15]

It is difficult to summarize accurately the detailed differences in personality among the three classes presented in this chapter. It may, nevertheless, be fairly correct to note that fewer evidences of personality maladjustment were found among upper class students, most among lower class students. Girls had fewer indications of personality deviation than did boys. Upper class girls, in particular, had an absence of deviant personality tendencies; their profile was similar to that of female college students.

[13] J. C. McKinley and S. R. Hathaway, "The Minnesota Multiphasic Personality Inventory: V. Hysteria, Hypomania, and Psychopathic Deviate," *Journal of Applied Psychology*, Vol. 28 (April, 1944), pp. 153-174. Hovey's study in which initiative, self-confidence and conscientiousness are associated with moderately high Ma scores in a student group is also pertinent. H. Birnet Hovey, "MMPI Profiles and Personality Characteristics," *Journal of Consulting Psychology*, Vol. 17 (April, 1953), pp. 142-146.
[14] Paul E. Meehl and Starke R. Hathaway, "The K Factor as a Suppressor Variable in the Minnesota Multiphasic Personality Inventory," *Journal of Applied Psychology*, Vol. 30 (October, 1946), pp. 525-564; Hathaway and Monachesi, *loc. cit.*, p. 107.
[15] The elevation of Mf scores with higher status subjects is most evident in the MMPI codes of college students; Goodstein, *loc. cit.*, Black, *loc. cit.*, and William C. Bier, "A Comparative Study of a Seminary Group and Four Other Groups on the Minnesota Multiphasic Personality Inventory," *Studies in Psychology and Psychiatry from the Catholic University of America*, Vol. 7 (April, 1948), pp. 1-107.

5

BROKEN HOMES, DEVIANCY,
AND PERSONALITY

$\mathcal{T}$ HERE IS fairly general agreement that behavior patterns
and personality structure are principally established during
the early formative years in the family.[1] By some, deviant
behavior is regarded as the result of inadequate training in
the home. By others, the family is viewed as a transmitter
of values and patterns of behavior, some of which are
deviant. In either instance, the pervasive force of the family
is evident and its disruption is a fact of consequence to
children and adolescents. The implications of this relationship of family inadequacy to deviant behavior are provoca-
tive; thus Bradley Buell reports that in St. Paul, "about 6

percent of the city's families, were suffering from such a compounding of serious problems that they were absorbing well over half of the combined services of the community's dependency, health, and adjustment agencies."[2]

One of the principal research needs in the study of family disruption is to trace the various patterns of adjustment and maladjustment among children from broken homes. We know that some children when confronted with an inadequate home situation turn to truancy or delinquency. But others do not. School failure is frequently associated with the indolence of parents. Yet some children rise above these circumstances to superior achievement. Clearly, there are alternative patterns of behavior which children follow when they find themselves within a deleterious home environment. It is the task of research to describe and analyze these alternative types of behavior and to delineate the corresponding personality configurations.

In the present chapter, ninth grade Kentucky students from broken homes are compared with their classmates who were from more stable homes. The purpose of the comparison and the subsequent analysis of personality is to ascertain which of various personal and social factors are most evidently associated with family disruption among adolescents. Such findings may provide an empirical framework for the further investigation of more precise relationships between personality, behavior, and deviant home environments.

[1] Gardner Murphy, *Personality* (New York: Harper and Brothers, 1947), chapter 37, "The Family as Mediator of Culture"; Kingsley Davis, *Human Society* (New York: The Macmillan Company, 1948), chapter 15, "Marriage and the Family"; Harry Stack Sullivan, *The Interpersonal Theory of Psychiatry* (New York: W. W. Norton and Company, 1953), chapter 7, "Infancy: Interpersonal Situations"; Eric Hamburger Erikson, "Growth and Crises of the 'Healthy Personality,'" *Personality in Nature, Society, and Culture*, Clyde Kluckhohn and Henry A. Murray, eds. (2nd ed. rev.; New York: Alfred A. Knopf, 1953), chapter 12; Talcott Parsons, *The Social System* (Glencoe, Illinois: The Free Press, 1951), chapter 7.

[2] Bradley Buell and Associates, *Community Planning for Human Services* (New York: Columbia University Press, 1952), p. 9.

CHARACTERISTICS OF STUDENTS
FROM BROKEN HOMES

Of the 200 ninth grade students, 16 percent were from homes broken by divorce, separation or death.[3] Of these 33 students, 12 were boys and 21 were girls. Ten of the 33 students from broken homes were Negroes.

There was no difference in mean age between the students from broken homes and those from stable homes (Table 17). With respect to social mobility, there was no association between Kentucky nativity or permanence of local residence and broken homes. The broken families were not more mobile in place of residence than the intact families.

The mean I.Q. of the boys from broken homes was 98.3 compared with a mean of 104.2 for the boys from stable homes. The mean I.Q.'s of the girls from broken and from stable homes were quite similar—103.1 and 104.5 respectively.

School grades were significantly lower among the boys from broken homes than among their classmates from stable homes. The former group had a grade average of 3.4 or D+, while the latter group received grades of 4.6 or C. Although this grade distribution is based upon small numbers, it is worth noting that one-third of the boys from broken homes received grades of D—, the lowest ranking received by any of the public school students. The grade distribution of the girls from broken homes was similar to that of the girls from stable homes.

Students from broken homes were somewhat more likely to be behind in grade level for their age. Of the boys from broken homes 50 percent were retarded in grade placement compared with 32 percent among the boys from stable homes. Comparable figures for the girls were 29 and 14 percent respectively for the broken and stable home groups.

[3] Nye found that 19.7 percent of the high school boys he studied came from broken homes; F. Ivan Nye, *Family Relationships and Delinquent Behavior* (New York: John Wiley and Sons, 1958), p. 44.

Table 17. Age, Nativity, Residential Mobility, Intelligence Quotient, School Grades, Educational Retardation, After-School Employment, and Socioeconomic Status of Students from Broken and from Stable Homes by Sex[a]

Group	N	Mean Age	Kentucky Nativity, Percent	Local Nativity, Percent	Mean I.Q.	Grade Average	Retarded in school, Percent	Percent Employed Part-Time	Lower Class, Percent
Boys from Broken Homes	12	15.1	83.3	58.3	98.3	3.4 D+*	50.0	33.3	41.7
Boys from Stable Homes	83	15.0	84.1	56.1	104.2	4.6 C	31.7	28.9	26.5
Girls from Broken Homes	21	14.8	90.5	61.9	103.1	5.1 C+	28.6	23.8*	47.4*
Girls from Stable Homes	84	14.8	91.5	64.6	104.5	5.1 C+	14.3	5.9	18.3

[a] Difference between boys, or girls, from broken and from stable homes was significant at level of: *P < .05; **P < .01. No test of significance applied to I.Q. data.

Girls from broken homes were more often employed after school hours than girls from stable homes. Of the first group some one-fourth (24 percent) were employed, while among the second group only 6 percent were employed. Among the boys, some one-third of each group held part-time jobs.

From Table 18 it is notable that the students from broken homes are disproportionately from the lower class. Correspondingly, only one upper class student is included with the broken home group. The broken home group, then, is to a considerable extent a subgroup of the lower class students who have, in addition to low socioeconomic status, unstable families.

Significant differences between the students from broken homes and those not from such homes were found with respect to academic achievement, after-school employment and socioeconomic status. Coming from homes broken by divorce, separation or death was not associated with appreciable differences in age, intelligence, or nativity.

MMPI PROFILES OF STUDENTS
FROM BROKEN HOMES

The boys from broken homes differed significantly in mean scores from the stable home boys on three MMPI scales—D, Ma, and Si. The most pronounced difference was on the Depression Scale. The boys from broken homes had a mean score some 12 points higher than boys from stable homes on this scale; this mean difference was significant beyond the .001 level. In addition to the higher Si score, the boys from broken homes were lower on Ma. This is the lowest Ma score for any group of boys in the entire study.

The girls from broken homes differed from those of stable homes only with respect to the L scale. The higher L scores of the broken home group are perhaps indicative of a slight "faking-good" tendency which is also suggested by the somewhat higher mean K score.

Table 18. Socioeconomic Status of Students from Broken and from Stable Homes as Ranked on the Minnesota Scale for Paternal Occupations

Socioeconomic Status		Boys				Girls*			
		Broken Homes		Stable Homes		Broken Homes		Stable Homes	
		Number	Percent	Number	Percent	Number	Percent	Number	Percent
Upper	1			8	9.6			7	8.5
	2			12	14.5	1	5.3	11	13.4
Middle	3	2	16.7	18	21.7	5	26.3	19	23.2
	4			1	1.2			4	4.9
	5	5	41.7	22	26.5	4	21.1	26	31.7
Lower	6	5	41.7	9	10.8	9	47.4	10	12.2
	7			13	15.7			5	6.1
Total		12	100.0	83	100.0	19	100.0	82	100.0

* Four cases omitted

Difference in socioeconomic status of students from broken and from stable homes: Boys $X^2 = 3.91$, $P < .20$; Girls $X^2 = 8.16$, $P < .02$.

The MMPI codes of the students from broken homes, as well as those from stable homes, were as follows:

	Boys	Girls
Broken Homes	274-80 5193 6/ F/LK ?:	49-8 763 05/21: FKL/?:
Stable Homes	9-48 76 5302 1/ F/KL ?:	49-8 76 0352/1: F K/L ?:

The code of the boys from broken homes delineates a personality pattern characterized by depression, lack of confidence in self, and asocial tendencies. In this regard the prominence of scale 2 and 7 is notable. Further, the lowness of scale 9—which, when moderately elevated in the present adolescent population, is commonly associated with successful or superior socialization—suggests a lack of youthful energy and lack of optimism on the part of the boys from broken homes, contrasted with those from stable homes.

The group MMPI codes of the girls from broken and stable homes are quite similar. No such marked differences as between the two groups of boys obtain for the girls.

It may be seen from the list of individual codes that the group personality patterns described are not a statistical artifact, but reflect the particular profiles of the subjects from broken homes. Thus, 50 percent of the boys from broken homes have codes in which scale 2 is first, contrasted with 8 percent of the boys from stable homes with such a pattern (see Table 12). With regard to scale 9, it is below a T-score of 60 among 75 percent of the boys from broken homes (see List of Codes).

Perusal of the individual MMPI codes of the girls from broken homes also suggests personality patterns comparable to the group code. In general, there is similarity between the girls from broken homes and those from stable homes in their personality patterns. The only exception noted is the frequency of scale 7 in the 70's (24 percent vs. 4 percent for the broken home and stable home groups), perhaps suggesting a higher incidence of worry or lack of confidence among the girls from broken homes.

69

Table 19. MMPI Mean Scale Scores, Standard Deviations, and t Values of Students from Broken Homes and from Stable Homes[a]

| | Boys | | | | | Girls | | | | |
| | Broken Homes N=12 | | Stable Homes N=83 | | t-Test | Broken Homes N=21 | | Stable Homes N=84 | | t-Test |
Scale	Mean	S.D.	Mean	S.D.		Mean	S.D.	Mean	S.D.	
?	6.4	9.11	6.8	11.26	1.066	1.8	2.76	3.4	9.12	0.814
L	3.8	1.83	3.5	2.08	0.419	4.8	2.01	3.8	1.99	2.011*
F	6.1	3.15	6.0	3.44	0.124	5.6	3.65	5.9	3.40	0.351
K	11.5	5.12	12.0	4.43	0.354	14.5	5.22	12.6	4.61	1.643
1 (Hs)	54.7	12.58	50.8	8.91	1.320	49.1	8.80	49.5	8.36	0.217
2 (D)	64.4	10.31	52.5	10.88	3.540**	49.2	8.22	51.3	8.21	1.048
3 (Hy)	53.6	7.53	52.7	6.51	0.444	52.4	9.57	52.9	8.84	0.220
4 (Pd)	60.7	4.70	59.6	9.56	0.388	61.3	9.13	61.0	10.57	0.136
5 (Mf)	54.8	5.26	53.4	8.30	0.591	50.1	6.25	51.9	9.02	0.849
6 (Pa)	52.3	3.90	54.5	9.23	0.840	55.2	9.24	56.3	9.77	0.450
7 (Pt)	62.3	8.71	57.8	10.36	1.442	57.9	8.04	57.1	8.58	0.365
8 (Sc)	59.2	7.40	59.3	10.58	0.050	59.6	8.59	59.9	9.74	1.523
9 (Ma)	53.8	7.75	63.5	10.86	2.938**	60.4	9.31	60.4	9.71	0.251
0 (Si)	59.0	8.95	52.7	8.64	2.309*	50.7	7.27	53.3	8.15	1.332

[a] Validity scales are reported in mean raw scores, clinical scales in mean T-scores. K corrections have been applied to scales 1, 4, 7, 8, and 9. Significance of differences between means: *P < .05; **P < .01.

DISCUSSION

The comparison of adolescents from broken homes with those whose home life is more stable reveals that personality maladjustment is more prevalent among the children from disrupted families. In itself this general finding might be anticipated since the impact of family life upon early socialization, including personality development, has received widespread theoretical recognition as well as considerable empirical substantiation.[4]

Yet, while there is general agreement on the pervasive importance of family life in the socialization process, the research findings taken together have been ambiguous and contradictory.[5] It seems likely that such ambiguities will be resolved as more comprehensive studies are undertaken, as standard instruments are employed, and as it becomes feasible to consider specific variables and diverse relationships within the family. In regard to this last point, it is pertinent to note that the comparison in the present chapter employed a gross criterion of family inadequacy. The mere fact of family disruption by divorce, separation, or death does not take into account the nature of the breakup—which may be beneficial. Further, this comparison does not consider the important question of the psychological or emotional adequacy of the home.[6] Admittedly, these factors are important.

[4] Robert F. Peck, "Family Patterns Correlated With Adolescent Personality Structure," *Journal of Abnormal and Social Psychology*, Vol. 57 (November, 1958), pp. 347-350; Robert D. Wirt and Peter F. Briggs, "Personality and Environmental Factors in Development of Delinquency," *Psychological Monographs*, Vol. 73, No. 15 (1959), pp. 1-47.

[5] See for example, Lee G. Burchinal, "Parents' Attitudes and Adjustment of Children," *Journal of Genetic Psychology*, Vol. 92 (March, 1958), pp. 69-79, and Harold Orlansky, "Infant Care and Personality," *Psychological Bulletin*, Vol. 46 (January, 1949), pp. 1-48.

[6] For a discussion of broken homes and the psychological adequacy of family life, see: Herbert A. Block and Frank T. Flynn, *Delinquency, The Juvenile Offender in America Today* (New York: Random House, 1956), pp. 181-187; Paul W. Tappan, *Crime, Justice and Correction* (New York: McGraw-Hill Book Co., 1960), chapter 8.

Boys (N=12)	Girls (N=21)
2'1478 3-96/05: (9:6:7:16)	34'17-6 28 90 5/ (3:9:2:21)
21'08 47-36/59: (3:2:8:7)	43-728 19/06 5: (0:9:4:21)
2'4 130-7 689/5: (27:6:9:11)	4 380/5796 12: (0:7:0:20)
2 781'49 35-6/0: (2:7:6:19)	48 79-52/610 3: (0:4:6:14)
27'80-6549/31: (4:1:11:3)	49'78 6 3/5 2 10: (2:2:3:13)
287 45-60 9/13: (1:3:11:9)	5-4870/93 62:1# (0:5:3:14)
4-3 2581/79 60: (25:2:3:18)	61 37 2'48-90/5: (3:5:7:18)
50-9 4678/213: (0:4:2:14)	7-3 468 1/925 0: (9:5:5:20)
7 1023 4-8 569/ (0:5:2:8)	74 68-931/2 50: (0:3:3:17)
79'0 28-54/63:1# (1:4:7:4)	7 86 9-24 50/13: (0:3:13:8)
9 04756 238/1: (5:2:3:13)	84'609-721/35: (1:3:13:10)
0'47-5 26 8/3 19: (0:3:4:16)	8-579 34/10 2:6# (7:3:3:15)
	89"476'0-25 13/ (0:2:12:7)
	9 4-6 0 3 /521: (0:6:10:5)
	94 7-5 8 26/1 30: (0:5:6:16)
	94-78 261 3/5 0: (0:7:2:22)
	9 48 6/73105:2# (8:3:4:19)
	9-6 84/570 32 1: (2:4:2:17)
	97-680 34 1/25: (0:7:7:14)
	9"8-43 6/70 15:2# (0:5:5:7)
	05 8-679/421 3: (2:4:7:7)

Still, the present data indicate that, whatever the association of factors extrinsic to the family and whatever the effect of less obvious or subtle relationships, family disruption itself has a pervasive impact upon adolescent personality. Particularly marked were the neurotic tendencies evident among boys from broken homes. On this basis one must at least question the common notion that broken homes are more disabling for girls than for boys. Does the girl from such a home view this disruption as less devastating to her personally? Are the girls already thinking of their own homes while the boys have no comparable goal in sight? These questions invite further study.

6

ACADEMIC FAILURE AND PERSONALITY

WHICH factors and conditions are associated with high and which with low performance in the educational system? Are high school students who are failing maladjusted in personality? Or are they from families of low socioeconomic status? Are there differences in failure rates between boys and girls? How do students who obtain superior school grades compare in personality and personal characteristics with those who receive average and failing grades? These are some of the questions considered in the present chapter.

Academic achievement has generally been considered to be dependent upon or related to intellectual ability,[1] personality characteristics,[2] or cultural factors.[3] The first two of these factors have most commonly been investigated by psychologists and the third by sociologists and, to a lesser extent, anthropologists. Determination of the relative impact of these factors (and others, such as the physiological) in specific social situations within specified populations at a given time is a task for empirical investigation. Here attention is directed toward background characteristics and personality configurations associated with academic success and failure among ninth grade high school students in Kentucky.

CHARACTERISTICS OF THE SUPERIOR, AVERAGE, AND FAILURE GROUPS

On the basis of academic performance in the previous semester, the ninth grade boys and girls were separated into three groups. The first group consisted of those students

[1] Four recent volumes, each with an extensive bibliography, which encompass this field may be cited: Kenneth Eells, *et al.*, *Intelligence and Cultural Differences* (Chicago: University of Chicago Press, 1951); John B. Miner, *Intelligence in the United States* (New York: Springer Publishing Company, 1957); Audrey Mary Shuey, *The Testing of Negro Intelligence* (Lynchburg, Virginia: J. P. Bell Company, 1958); David Wechsler, *The Measurement and Appraisal of Adult Intelligence*, 4th ed. (Baltimore: The Williams and Wilkins Company, 1958).

[2] Gordon W. Allport, *Personality* (New York: Henry Holt and Company, 1937); David C. McClelland *et al.*, *The Achievement Motive* (New York: Appleton-Century-Crofts, 1953).

[3] A diversity of cultural factors, including socioeconomic status, ethnic group membership, rural-urban differences, and value orientations, have been related to academic achievement. For examples, see August B. Hollingshead, *Elmtown's Youth* (New York: John Wiley and Sons, 1949); Fred L. Strodtbeck, "Family Interaction, Values, and Achievement," *Talent and Society*, David C. McClelland, *et al.*, eds. (Princeton: D. Van Nostrand Company, 1958), chapter 4; Herbert H. Hyman, "The Value Systems of Different Classes: A Social Psychological Contribution to the Analysis of Stratification," *Class, Status and Power*, Reinhard Bendix and Seymour Martin Lipset, eds. (Glencoe, Illinois: The Free Press, 1953), pp. 426-442; James S. Coleman, *The Adolescent Society* (New York: The Free Press of Glencoe, 1961).

74

who had achieved an A or B grade average. The second group had C averages, while the third had a D or E average. These groups were designated as high, average and low in achievement. Of the 200 ninth grade students with valid MMPI profiles, school grades were available for 196. Of these, 39.8 percent were high achievers, 48.0 percent were average achievers, and 12.2 percent were low achievers.

The girls received somewhat higher grades than the boys. Among the 93 boys, 34.4 percent received high grades, 47.3 percent average grades, and 18.3 percent low or failing grades. Among the 103 girls, 44.7 percent achieved high grades, 48.5 percent average grades, and only 6.8 percent had low grades.

The mean age of the 32 high achievement boys was 14.9 years; for the 44 in the average group and 17 in the low group, mean ages were both 15.1 years. Among the girls, the respective mean ages of the high, average, and low groups were 14.7, 14.8, and 14.9 years. The age of the superior groups was slightly lower, as expected, but the failure groups were not notably older, as might have been anticipated.

Residential mobility was associated with academic success. Of the boys with high grades, 62.5 percent were not born in their town of present residence, compared with 36.4 percent of the average and 29.4 percent of the low achievers. For the girls, corresponding percentages were 46.7, 28.6, and 14.3 in the superior, average, and low group.

Race was also associated with academic achievement. Of the 14 Negro boys, 2 were in the high achievement group, 4 in the average, and 8 in the low group. Of the 17 Negro girls, 3 were high achievers, 11 average, and 3 low achievers. In the high achievement group, 7 percent were Negro students; in the low achievement group, 49 percent were Negroes.

Mean I.Q. scores of the high, average, and low achievement boys were 106.9, 102.7 and 95.0 respectively. Comparable figures for the girls were 111.8, 97.9, and 91.0. The greater difference of means among the girls probably reflects

Table 20. Number of Years Students With High, Average, and Low Grades Were Retarded in Grade Placement[a]

Years Retarded	Boys						Girls					
	High		Average		Low		High		Average		Low	
	N	Pct.	N	Pct.	N	Pct.	N	Pct.	N	Pct.	N	Pct.
0	26	81.3	28	63.6	7	41.2	45	97.8	36	72.0	4	57.1
1	6	18.8	12	27.3	8	47.1	1	2.2	12	24.0	3	42.9
2			2	4.5	2	11.8			2	4.0		
3 or 4			2	4.5								
Total	32	100.0	44	100.0	17	100.0	46	100.0	50	100.0	7	100.0

[a] Four cases omitted; two boys and two girls

Difference in grade retardation by achievement levels: Boys $X^2 = 8.04$, P < .02; Girls $X^2 = 14.45$, P < .001.

higher educational motivation in that girls with high I.Q.'s were less likely to be average achievers.

As anticipated, achievement was inversely associated with educational retardation. The boys were more retarded in grade placement than the girls, even when the sexes were equated for achievement. For the sexes combined, 9.0 percent of the high achievement students were retarded one or more years, while 31.9 percent of the average achievers and 54.2 percent of the low achievers were similarly retarded (see Table 20).

Work outside of school was not associated with either academic success or failure. Among the high, average, and low achievement boys 25.0, 34.1, and 29.4 percent were employed. Among the girls, corresponding percentages were 4.3, 14.0, and 14.3 for the three groups. There were more high achievement boys engaged in delivery jobs (mostly paper routes) than was the case in the average or low groups. Otherwise, type of work did not vary with achievement.

The percentage of the high achievement boys who lived in homes broken by divorce, separation or death was 9.4. For the average and low achievers the percentage of boys who came from such homes was 9.1 and 29.4. For the girls, the corresponding percentages were 17.4, 22.0, and 14.3.

Poor academic performance was associated with lower class status. Within the failure group, 61 percent of the students were from the lower class; yet most of the lower class children were not failures. Only 28 percent were in this category (Table 21). In addition, academic failure was uncommon among the upper class students and high grades were frequently obtained. Thus, only 5 percent of the upper class students were receiving failing grades, while 61 percent of this group were high achievers.

In comparing the background characteristics of high school students who were above average, average and below average in academic achievement it was found that age was not related to achievement. For the boys, parental mobility was more common among the high achievers, but this

Table 21. Socioeconomic Status of Students with High, Average, and Low School Grades

Socio-economic Status	Boys						Girls*					
	High Grades		Average Grades		Low Grades		High Grades		Average Grades		Low Grades	
	N	Pct.	N	Pct.	N	Pct.	N	Pct.	N	Pct.	N	Pct.
Upper 1	3	9.4	4	9.1			5	11.1	2	4.2		
2	8	25.0	3	6.8	1	5.9	7	15.6	4	8.3	1	16.7
3	8	25.0	10	22.7	2	11.8	11	24.4	12	25.0		
Middle 4							2	4.4	2	4.2		
5	6	18.8	18	40.9	3	17.6	14	31.1	14	29.2	2	33.3
Lower 6	3	9.4	4	9.1	7	41.2	4	8.9	12	25.0	2	33.3
7	4	12.5	5	11.4	4	23.5	2	4.4	2	4.2	1	16.7
Total	32	100.0	44	100.0	17	100.0	45	100.0	48	100.0	6	100.0

* Four cases omitted

Difference in socioeconomic status by achievement levels: Boys $X^2 = 17.63$, $P < .01$; Girls $X^2 = 7.60$, $P < .20$.

appears to reflect differences in socioeconomic status. Two findings seem of outstanding significance. The first was the superior achievement of the girls. Not only were the girls more often high achievers, but they infrequently were low achievers; 74 percent of the failure group were male. Secondly, the association of grade average with socioeconomic status was apparent. It is crucial to note, however, that although those students who received failing grades were predominantly from lower status homes, most of the students from such homes were not failures. Differential academic achievement, then, is apparent among these students.

ACADEMIC ACHIEVEMENT AND MMPI PROFILES

The ninth grade boys differed significantly on three MMPI scales when they were grouped by school achievement. The low achievers had a higher mean score on Hs than either of the other groups of boys. Indeed, the low group was more than 10 points above the high group; this mean difference was significant beyond the .001 level. Secondly, the low achievers were higher on the D scale. And thirdly, the low achievement group was higher on the F scale.

Among the girls, there were significant differences on 10 of the 14 scales. The high achievement group was lower in mean scores than either of the other groups on scales 2, 5, and 8, and F; they were higher on K. In addition, the average girls were significantly higher in mean scores than the high achievers on scales 4, 6, 9, and 0. The low achievers were higher than either group on the Cannot Say Scale.

The MMPI codes of these six achievement groups were:

	Boys	Girls
High Grades	9-8 47 056 32/1: F/KL ?:	49 87 63 0/5 12: KF/L?:
Average Grades	94-87 6325 01/ F/LK ?:	498-76 0 253 1/F-L/K?:
Low Grades	798-241 603 5/ F-KL ?:	8 5-4 6 790 2/31: F-L/K?:

79

Table 22. MMPI Mean Scale Scores, Standard Deviations, and t Values of Boys with High, Average, and Low Academic Achievement[a]

Scale	High Achievement N=32		Average Achievement N=44		Low Achievement N=17		t-Test High-Average	t-Test High-Low	t-Test Average-Low
	Mean	S.D.	Mean	S.D.	Mean	S.D.			
?	7.5	14.79	5.9	7.25	8.2	10.95	0.602	0.163	0.915
L	3.3	2.09	3.7	2.04	3.4	2.09	0.697	0.106	0.453
F	5.2	3.30	6.0	3.37	7.6	3.07	0.976	2.491*	1.775
K	11.9	4.95	12.2	3.73	11.0	5.44	0.349	0.557	0.987
1 (Hs)	47.6	8.07	51.2	8.86	58.2	10.43	1.781	3.864**	2.598*
2 (D)	50.4	11.25	53.7	10.15	59.4	11.88	1.315	2.553*	1.837
3 (Hy)	51.3	6.50	53.8	6.70	53.5	6.56	1.605	1.111	0.144
4 (Pd)	57.8	9.02	61.3	9.23	59.0	8.37	1.643	0.452	0.887
5 (Mf)	54.5	8.28	53.6	8.05	51.9	7.30	0.446	1.037	0.734
6 (Pa)	53.8	9.17	54.7	9.12	53.6	7.36	0.411	0.097	0.453
7 (Pt)	57.5	10.20	57.8	10.30	61.4	9.18	0.113	1.275	1.233
8 (Sc)	59.3	9.61	58.7	10.33	60.2	10.00	0.271	0.298	0.515
9 (Ma)	62.9	10.71	63.0	9.64	61.1	13.33	0.036	0.524	0.627
0 (Si)	54.6	10.17	52.5	7.87	53.6	8.72	1.005	0.308	0.506

[a] Validity scales are reported in mean raw scores, clinical scales in mean T-scores. K corrections have been applied to scales 1, 4, 7, 8, and 9. Significance of differences between means: *P < .05; **P < .01.

The personality of the boys in the superior or high group is characterized by the prominence of energetic tendencies and the absence of neurotic trends. In the code, scale 9 is dominant and scales 3, 2, and 1 are low. Among the boys with average grades the energy of scale 9 is combined with the aggressiveness or unconventionality indicated by scale 4. The code delineates a personality type which is somewhat more rebellious and socially inept than that of the high achievement boys. The code of the low achievement boys is markedly different from either of the others. The prominence of scales 7 and 8 as well as the elevation of 2 and 1 indicates excessive worry, lack of confidence, withdrawal tendencies and neurotic traits. In this regard the dominance of scale 7 seems especially significant, for this is the only MMPI group code beginning with Pt in the study.

The code and profile of the high achievement girls delineates a personality which is similar to that of college females. None of the clinical scales is in the T-score 60 range. Further, the lowness of the neurotic scales is evident. Among the girls whose achievement was average, energetic and mildly aggressive tendencies are combined with increased sensitivity. This is seen in the elevation of the Sc scale along with Pd and Ma. In addition, neurotic tendencies—particularly on scale 2—are somewhat more apparent. The code of the girls with poorest grades characterized a personality in which interpersonal difficulties were prominent. The elevation of scale 8 combined with the decreased influence of scale 9 suggests apathetic trends as well as lack of energy and unsociability.

DISCUSSION

Previous studies with the MMPI which have undertaken to assay the relationship of personality to academic achievement have presented inconclusive or contradictory findings. When the selectiveness and diversity of the American educational system is taken into account, much of the apparent am-

81

Table 23. MMPI Mean Scale Scores, Standard Deviations, and t Values of Girls with High, Average, and Low Academic Achievement[a]

Scale	High Achievement N=46		Average Achievement N=50		Low Achievement N=7		t-Test High-Average	t-Test High-Low	t-Test Average-Low
	Mean	S.D.	Mean	S.D.	Mean	S.D.			
?	2.2	3.45	2.2	4.50	15.4	25.32	0.045	3.277**	3.283**
L	3.7	1.55	4.3	2.38	4.1	2.10	1.245	0.597	0.121
F	3.7	2.24	7.3	3.44	8.4	2.72	5.860**	4.929**	0.847
K	14.7	4.63	11.5	4.46	10.9	3.83	3.428**	2.058*	0.356
1 (Hs)	47.7	8.19	50.4	7.88	48.9	5.22	1.670	0.371	0.500
2 (D)	47.3	7.80	53.3	7.42	53.7	5.82	3.795**	2.048*	0.153
3 (Hy)	52.7	8.80	52.8	8.93	49.7	8.08	0.023	0.833	0.840
4 (Pd)	57.9	8.80	63.6	10.63	59.7	8.61	2.781**	0.490	0.900
5 (Mf)	48.9	7.89	53.0	8.44	60.0	6.21	2.409*	3.494**	2.090*
6 (Pa)	53.2	8.56	58.1	9.55	58.0	10.14	2.615*	1.329	0.020
7 (Pt)	55.8	8.54	58.2	8.26	56.9	7.08	1.406	0.311	0.408
8 (Sc)	56.6	6.38	62.1	10.60	63.6	12.42	3.000**	2.256*	0.335
9 (Ma)	57.9	8.24	63.0	9.70	56.3	11.98	2.740**	0.446	1.638
0 (Si)	50.2	7.47	54.8	8.32	55.4	5.47	2.818**	1.764	0.203

[a] Validity scales are reported in mean raw scores, clinical scales in mean T-scores. K corrections have been applied to scales 1, 4, 7, 8, and 9. Significant of differences between means: $*P < .05$; $**P < .01$.

biguity in MMPI studies of academic achievement may be dispelled. The lack of differentiation of the MMPI scales with respect to high school seniors of high and low achievement, reported by Gough,[4] is not unexpected. Comparison of both male and female profiles in the present Kentucky study with those reported by Hathaway and Monachesi for Minnesota ninth graders[5] supports the contention that a similar selectivity with respect to personality factors is operative in the two areas.

With respect to college samples, both the overall similarity of MMPI profiles generally reported[6] and such exceptions as studies of overachievers and underachievers[7] are consistent with the interpretation here offered. In the former instance, the greater selectivity of colleges compared with public schools would be expected to appear in less profile variation. Secondly, it might be anticipated that

[4] Harrison G. Gough, "Factors Relating to the Academic Achievement of High-School Students," *Journal of Educational Psychology*, Vol. 40 (February, 1949), pp. 65-78.

[5] Starke R. Hathaway and Elio D. Monachesi, "Personality Characteristics of Adolescents as Related to Their Later Careers," *Analyzing and Predicting Juvenile Delinquency with the MMPI*, Hathaway and Monachesi, eds. (Minneapolis: University of Minnesota Press, 1953), pp. 87-135 (Studies 6 and 7).

[6] J. D. Black, "MMPI Results for Fifteen Groups of Female College Students," *Basic Readings on the MMPI in Psychology and Medicine*, G. S. Welsh and W. Grant Dahlstrom, eds. (Minneapolis: University of Minnesota Press, 1956), pp. 562-573; Leonard D. Goodstein, "Regional Differences in MMPI Responses Among Male College Students," *Journal of Consulting Psychology*, Vol. 18 (December, 1954), pp. 437-441.

[7] See, for example, Henry H. Morgan, "A Psychometric Comparison of Achieving and Nonachieving College Students of High Ability," *Journal of Consulting Psychology*, Vol. 16 (August, 1952), pp. 292-298; William D. Altus, "A College Achiever and Non-Achiever Scale for the Minnesota Multiphasic Personality Inventory," *Journal of Applied Psychology*, Vol. 32 (August, 1948), pp. 385-397; William A. Owens and Wilma C. Johnson, "Some Measured Personality Traits of Collegiate Underachievers," *Journal of Educational Psychology*, Vol. 40 (January, 1949), pp. 41-46; Donald H. Kausler and E. Philip Trapp, "Relationship Between Achievement Motivation Scores and Manifest Anxiety Scores," *Journal of Consulting Psychology*, Vol. 22 (December, 1958), pp. 448-450.

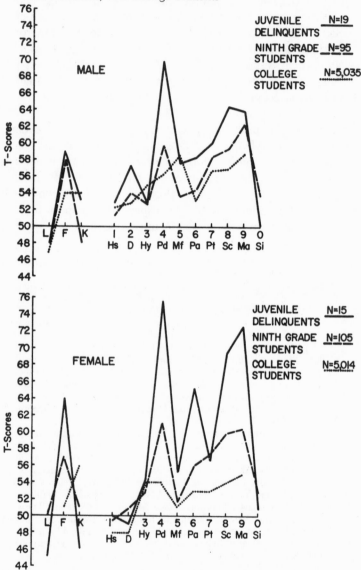

Figure 2. MMPI Profiles of Incarcerated Delinquents, Ninth Grade Students, and College Students

Source: Text, Table 5; *Basic Readings on the MMPI in Psychology and Medicine,* pp. 257, 565, 576.

seminary students or nurses would differ from liberal arts or commerce students. And such is the case.[8]

In Figure 2 the profiles of high school students and college students are presented against the test norms for adults. College students have profiles which are midway between the test norms—T of 50—and those of the high school subjects on many of the scales. Figure 2 shows that the personality profiles completed by high school students differ from those completed by college students.

The profile differences between high and low achievers reported in the present study approximate the differences obtained between college students and high school students who did not continue their studies. Hathaway, Monachesi, and Erickson found that the noncontinuing students were more deviant in behavior and attitudes than the university students. The MMPI codes of their university and noncontinuing groups were as follows:[9]

	Male	Female
University Students	984 7 56 310/2: FK/L:	485 7609/3 21: KL/F:
Noncontinuing Students	489-7 061235/ F-K/L:	984 57 60/3 12: FK/L:

The similarity of these Minnesota group differences to the ninth grade Kentucky differences in achievement groups is seen in the greater profile elevation of the noncontinuing and lower achievement subjects. Further, the prominence of the Sc scale in the low achievement groups and the higher F scores than among high achievers is evident in both studies.

It was found, then, that the Kentucky high school

8 William C. Bier, "A Comparative Study of a Seminary Group and Four Other Groups on the Minnesota Multiphasic Personality Inventory," *Studies in Psychology and Psychiatry from the Catholic University of America,* Vol. 7 (April, 1948), pp. 1-107; H. Birnet Hovey, "MMPI Aberration Potentials in a Nonclinical Group," *Journal of Social Psychology,* Vol. 40 (November, 1954), pp. 299-307.

9 Starke R. Hathaway, Elio D. Monachesi, and Mary Lee Erickson, "Relationship of College Attendance to Personality Characteristics and Early Delinquent Behavior," *The Sociological Quarterly,* Vol. 1 (April, 1960), p. 104.

students who were superior in their academic performance had personality patterns which are most similar to those of college students while the failing ninth graders were most dissimilar. Definite personality patterns were associated with superior achievement in high school, and these personality patterns were comparable with those for university students. Concomitantly, high school failure was related to personality maladjustment, and these personality patterns were somewhat similar—in configuration, but not in elevation—to those reported for clinical groups.

7

THE TEACHER, STUDENT DEVIANCE
AND PERSONALITY

THE PROBLEM of social deviancy within the educational system involves a consideration of the extent and nature of student deviance in behavior and attitudes in addition to the question of academic failure and its ramifications. How common are behavioral problems among ninth graders? What do teachers regard as personality maladjustment? Are the teachers able to identify those students who are deviant? How important is socioeconomic background of students in relation to classroom behavior and personality?

Attention in the present chapter is directed along two lines of inquiry: First, ascertainment of the background

characteristics and personality patterns of those students
whom teachers regarded as effecting unsatisfactory social or
personality adjustment in school; second, determination of
the validity of teachers' opinions with respect to student
personality by comparing their judgments with MMPI
results.

THE TEACHERS' RATINGS

There were ten ninth grade teachers in the two high schools
from which the students of this study were selected. Six of
these teachers were women and four were men. Each of the
ten homeroom teachers rated the students in his class with
respect to personality and problem behavior. There were
224 boys and girls in attendance at the time the MMPI was
administered. Ratings were obtained for 222 of these students; a rating was not completed for two students who had
recently enrolled in school. In considering the teachers'
ratings, the 24 students who completed invalid MMPI
profiles are combined with the 200 students with valid
profiles since the purpose is analysis of teachers' opinions
and knowledge of all students.

Each teacher ranked his students on a four-point scale
of personality adjustment. The ranks were: (1) exceptionally well adjusted, (2) average personality adjustment,
(3) below average, and (4) far below average. In addition,
the teacher was asked whether the student displayed antisocial attitudes, had been a disciplinary problem in school,
engaged in truancy during the school year, or had been in
difficulty with the law or other authorities outside of school.

This rating procedure, admittedly, has its limitations.
Particularly, it might be anticipated that the ratings provided
would depend in large part upon the disposition and attitudes
of the teacher himself. Still, these very dispositions are a
part of the school situation encountered by the adolescent
student and, therefore, are pertinent to this study. It is not
assumed that the teachers' ratings have any psychological or

psychiatric validity other than in the social situational sense already indicated. Rather this relationship of teacher judgment of personality to psychological and social data is itself the object of investigation.

From Table 24 it may be seen that the most common personality rating by teachers was "average personality adjustment." This rating—category 2—was applied to 50.9 percent of the students. Of the remainder, 30.2 percent were rated above average, 17.1 percent below average, and 1.8 percent far below average in personality adjustment. There was considerable variation among the teachers in their rating as well as certain similarities. Seven of the ten teachers placed more of their students in the average category than either above or below average. For two teachers the modal category was "exceptionally well adjusted" (teachers 9 and 10 in Table 24), while one rated half of his students (but there were only eight in this class) as below average in personality adjustment. Nine of the 10 teachers rated some students as exceptionally well adjusted, while all 10 rated some below average or far below average. Considerable teacher variation is evident in the percentage of class rated maladjusted in personality (that is, rated either below or far below average in personality adjustment). From 50 to 70 percent of particular classes were rated as maladjusted (Table 24). This variation in personality rating may be the result of actual differences in class composition, or to diverse standards of judgment among the teachers, or to a combination of these two factors. Interestingly, there was no evidence of differences between the male and female teachers in their ratings.

Of the 13 students designated by their teachers as behavior problems, five were antisocial in attitudes and disposition, nine were disciplinary problems in school, and five had been truant. None were reported to have had trouble with authorities outside of school. With regard to personality, 10 of the 13 were rated below average or far below average; none were rated exceptionally well adjusted.

Table 24. Teachers' Ratings of Students in Each Classroom with Respect to Personality Adjustment and Behavior Characteristics[a]

Teacher	Personality Rating				Total in Class	Rated 3 or 4		Number of Students Rated A, P or T
	1	2	3	4		Number	Percent of Class	
1	2	2	4		8	4	50.0	1
2	7	12	5	2	26	7	26.9	1
3	5	9	1		15	1	6.7	1
4	9	15	2	1	27	3	11.1	1
5		20	6		26	6	23.1	0
6	6	11	8	1	26	9	34.6	1
7	9	13	2		24	2	8.3	2
8	6	12	5		23	5	21.7	4
9	13	10	2		25	2	8.0	0
10	10	9	3		22	3	13.6	2
Total	67	113	38	4	222*	42	18.9	13

[a] Under Personality Rating, 1 refers to a rating by teacher of exceptionally well adjusted, 2 to average adjustment, 3 to below-average adjustment, and 4 to far-below-average adjustment. In last column, A refers to a rating of antisocial, P to problem in school, and T to truancy.

* Two cases omitted. Table includes students who completed invalid MMPI profiles as well as the valid group, since the purpose of the presentation is depiction of teacher variation in ratings.

Hence, most of the children considered to be behavior problems were also regarded as maladjusted in personality.

It is relevant to note that none of the 12 boys who were known to have been in difficulty with the police or courts were so identified by his teacher. Five of these 12 boys with delinquency records were identified as maladjusted in personality, while two of the five were also rated as antisocial in attitude and as disciplinary problems.

To summarize, the teachers agreed that the majority of their students have average or above-average personality adjustment. From a statistical viewpoint they appear to be even more consistent in designating a portion of their students as maladjusted. In addition to rating 18.9 percent of the students as maladjusted in personality, they rated 5.9 as behavior problems in school, truants, or as evidencing antisocial attitudes. Most of this latter group they also rated maladjusted in personality. Thus, the teachers considered personality difficulties more prevalent than behavior problems. This is even more clearly the case when it is noted that the antisocial attitude category is perhaps more of a personality than a behavioral designation. In addition to considering personality maladjustment some three times as prevalent as behavior problems, the teachers believed that the students with problems of behavior had unsatisfactory personalities.

CHARACTERISTICS OF THE MALADJUSTED STUDENTS

Of the 200 students with valid MMPI profiles, 22 boys and 12 girls were rated by their homeroom teachers as possessing one or more attributes indicative of unsatisfactory school adjustment. These 34 ninth graders constitute the sample for the comparative analysis of this chapter. This sample includes those students who were rated as unsatisfactory in personality adjustment as well as those rated as school problems. The latter group, however, was essentially a sub-group of the former, since all but one of the students

91

Table 25. Teachers' Ratings of Personality Adjustment of Male and Female Students

Personality Rating	Boys		Girls		Total	
	Number	Percent	Number	Percent	Number	Percent
Exceptionally Well Adjusted	24	25.3	39	37.5	63	31.7
Average Adjustment	50	52.6	53	51.0	103	51.8
Below-Average Adjustment	19	20.0	12	11.5	31	15.6
Far-Below-Average Adjustment	2	2.1			2	1.0
Total	95	100.0	104*	100.0	199	100.0

* One case omitted
Difference in teachers' ratings between boys and girls: $X^2 = 5.73$, $P < .10$.

92

designated as school problems were also rated unsatisfactory in personality. In sum, then, these 34 were the students whom the teachers regarded as failing to make a satisfactory adjustment to the school situation.

Of the 200 ninth graders, 52 percent were rated as having average personality adjustment. Of the remainder, 32 percent were rated above average, 16 percent below average, and 1 percent far below average in personality adjustment (see Table 25). The girls received more "exceptionally well-adjusted" ratings than the boys. In turn, the boys were designated twice as frequently as below average in personality—22 percent vs. 12 percent. Not only were more boys than girls identified as having personality deficiencies or difficulties, but the boys were more often ranked by their teachers as disciplinary problems and as possessing antisocial attitudes.

The mean age of the 22 maladjusted boys was 15.0 years, that of the maladjusted girls 14.8 years. The non-problem boys and girls had similar mean ages of 15.0 and 14.8 respectively.

There was no evidence that place of nativity was associated with poor school adjustment. Of the maladjusted boys, 62 percent were born in their town of present residence. Among the maladjusted girls, non-problem boys, and non-problem girls the comparable percentages were 58, 55, and 66 respectively.

Among the 34 problem children, 17.6 percent were Negro (13.6 percent of the boys and 25.0 percent of the girls). The Negro students as a group, then, were rated by their teachers as having approximately the same percentage of maladjusted pupils as the whole group.

The students rated as maladjusted by their teachers had lower I.Q. scores than did the non-problem students. The mean I.Q. of the maladjusted boys was 95.9. For the maladjusted girls, non-problem boys, and non-problem girls the respective mean I.Q.'s were 93.3, 105.2, and 105.3.

The maladjusted boys and girls were more retarded in

93

Table 26. Semester Grade Average of Students Rated as Maladjusted and as Adjusted by Their Teachers[a]

Semester Grade Average	Boys				Girls			
	Maladjusted		Adjusted		Maladjusted		Adjusted	
	Number	Percent	Number	Percent	Number	Percent	Number	Percent
8. (A)			4	5.6			3	3.3
7. (B+)	2	9.5	8	11.1			19	20.9
6. (B)	1	4.8	17	23.6			23	25.3
5. (C+)	1	4.8	12	16.7	4	36.4	16	17.6
4. (C)	3	14.3	16	22.2	2	18.2	16	17.6
3. (C−)	5	23.8	7	9.7	3	27.3	9	9.9
2. (D)	6	28.6	5	6.9	2	18.2	4	4.4
1. (D−)	3	14.3	3	4.2			1	1.1
0. (E)								
Total	21	100.0	72	100.0	11	100.0	91	100.0
Mean Grade	3.19		4.83		3.73		5.22	

[a] Five cases omitted; two boys and three girls

Significance of difference in grades between students rated as maladjusted and those rated as adjusted: Boys $t = 3.73$, $P < .001$; Girls $t = 3.01$, $P < .01$.

grade placement than the non-problem students. Of the maladjusted boys, 47.6 percent were retarded one or more years. Among the maladjusted girls, non-problem boys, and non-problem girls the comparable percentages were 33.3, 30.1, and 15.2. It may be noted that these differences were less than those observed with regard to social class (Chapter IV).

Academic achievement was more closely associated with school maladjustment ratings than was retardation. From Table 26 it may be seen that the maladjusted students were some four times as likely to be failing (i.e., making a grade average of D or E) as were the non-problem students. Correspondingly, they were less frequently above average students: 9 percent of the maladjusted students received grades of B or A compared with 45 percent of their non-problem classmates.

The maladjusted students were not, as a group, more often from broken homes than the non-problem students. For the maladjusted boys, maladjusted girls, non-problem boys, and non-problem girls the respective percentages from broken homes were 22.7, 16.7, 9.6, and 20.7.

The percentages of the four groups who worked outside of school hours were not notably different. The type of work was also quite similar within these four groups.

Differences in socioeconomic status between the two groups of students are presented in Table 27. It shows that 41 percent of the maladjusted students were from the lower class and only 6 percent from the upper class. Of all lower class students, 27 percent were rated as maladjusted while only 5 percent of the upper class were so rated. Among the maladjusted boys, 45 percent came from lower class homes.

In sum, those students whom teachers considered maladjusted in school were characterized by lower intelligence quotients, more educational retardation, poorer academic achievement, and lower socioeconomic status. Particularly marked was the poor academic performance and lower socioeconomic status of the maladjusted boys.

95

Table 27. Socioeconomic Status of Students Rated as Maladjusted and as Adjusted by Their Teachers

Socioeconomic Status		Boys				Girls			
		Maladjusted		Adjusted		Maladjusted		Adjusted	
Class	Status	Number	Percent	Number	Percent	Number	Percent	Number	Percent
Upper	1			8	11.0			7	8.0
	2	1	4.5	11	15.1	1	8.3	11	12.5
Middle	3	2	9.1	18	24.7	4	33.3	20	22.7
	4	1	4.5					4	4.5
	5	8	36.4	19	26.0	3	25.0	26	29.5
Lower	6	4	18.2	10	13.7	4	33.3	15	17.0
	7	6	27.3	7	9.6			5	5.7
Total		22	100.0	73	100.0	12	100.0	88*	100.0

* Four cases omitted

Difference in socioeconomic status between students rated as maladjusted and those rated as adjusted: Boys $X^2 = 6.63$, $P < .05$; Girls $X^2 = 1.32$, $P < .70$.

MMPI PROFILES OF THE
MALADJUSTED STUDENTS

In comparing the MMPI profiles of those students rated as maladjusted by their teachers with those who were not so rated, one finds significant differences between the two groups of boys with respect to scales 1, 2, 4, 5, and 8. The 22 maladjusted boys had higher mean scores on the Hs, D, Pd, and Sc scales, but the boys rated as average or better in adjustment were higher on Mf. Although just below the 5 percent confidence level, the higher K score of the maladjusted boys was surprising. Similarly, the higher Ma score of the better adjusted boys seems worthy of note.

Among the girls, those rated as maladjusted were significantly different from the adjusted group in mean score only on the F scale. This difference as well as the somewhat lower K score for the maladjusted girls suggests less defensiveness in addition to personality maladjustment.

The MMPI codes of the four group means presented in **Table 28** were:

	Boys	Girls
Maladjusted	48 72-9 163 05/ FK/L?:	9-4 786 02 35/1: F-L/K?:
Adjusted	9-487 560 32/1: F/KL ?:	489-76 305 2/1: F KL/?:

The code of the boys rated as maladjusted delineates a group personality profile which is more elevated than that of the adjusted boys. The prominence of scales 7 and 2 along with 4 and 8 in the 60 range suggests that unconventionality is combined with neurotic tendencies and sensitivity. The lack of optimism associated with high D and Pt as well as the decline in social energy associated with the low Ma lend further support to this interpretation. From the list of individual codes, it may be seen that scale 2 is higher than scale 9 among half of the maladjusted boys. This configuration of 2>9 seems to be particularly indicative of personality maladjustment among adolescent boys.

97

Table 28. MMPI Mean Scale Scores, Standard Deviations, and t Values of Students Rated as Maladjusted and Adjusted by Their Teachers[a]

| | Boys | | | | | Girls | | | | | |
| | Maladjusted N=22 | | Adjusted N=73 | | t-Test | Maladjusted N=12 | | Adjusted N=92 | | t-Test | |
Scale	Mean	S.D.	Mean	S.D.		Mean	S.D.	Mean	S.D.	
?	9.3	10.81	6.0	11.00	1.229	0.5	0.65	3.5	8.77	1.156
L	3.9	2.44	3.4	1.91	0.902	4.3	2.09	4.0	2.03	0.562
F	6.4	3.34	5.8	3.42	0.686	8.1	2.60	5.5	3.45	2.479*
K	13.0	5.13	11.6	4.27	1.254	10.4	4.42	13.3	4.77	1.971
1 (Hs)	55.7	9.19	49.9	9.23	2.563*	49.4	9.26	49.4	8.38	0.001
2 (D)	60.3	11.77	52.1	10.74	3.033**	54.2	6.56	50.6	8.35	1.427
3 (Hy)	54.8	5.00	52.2	6.96	1.647	51.7	7.51	52.9	9.20	0.430
4 (Pd)	64.1	8.95	58.4	8.72	2.647**	59.8	9.68	61.2	10.42	0.465
5 (Mf)	50.5	8.07	54.5	7.74	2.064*	51.7	5.12	51.8	8.77	0.032
6 (Pa)	55.7	5.47	53.8	9.50	0.866	57.7	9.44	55.8	9.73	0.620
7 (Pt)	61.2	10.44	57.5	10.07	1.483	58.1	10.05	57.1	8.25	0.392
8 (Sc)	63.4	9.42	58.1	10.14	2.177*	57.8	10.47	60.2	9.41	0.785
9 (Ma)	58.5	10.71	63.4	10.82	1.867	61.8	8.78	60.1	9.72	0.586
0 (Si)	53.3	9.02	53.6	8.89	0.157	54.9	5.06	52.6	8.29	0.937

[a] Validity scales are reported in mean raw scores, clinical scales in mean T-scores. K corrections have been applied to scales 1, 4, 7, 8, and 9. Significance of differences between means: *P < .05; **P < .01.

98

Among the girls, less marked code differences between the two groups were evident. The codes are quite similar, although the somewhat more elevated code of the adjusted group is surprising. Indeed, for the girls rated as maladjusted, only the higher F scale suggests personality deficiency.

DISCUSSION

Perhaps the most obvious initial fact about the students was that more boys than girls were judged to be maladjusted by their teachers. In this respect the teachers appear to be corroborating the findings of greater conformity or social sophistication among the girls.[1] Of the 200 students, 14.4 percent of the girls and 23.2 percent of the boys were rated as personality or school problems.

The association of academic achievement with teachers' ratings was pronounced. Thus, 66.7 percent of the maladjusted boys and 45.5 percent of the girls have grades below C. By comparison only 20.8 percent of the non-maladjusted boys and 15.4 percent of the girls had such grade averages (Table 26). Socioeconomic status, previous retardation in grade, and family stability were of lesser importance. It seems that the teachers employed classroom behavior and performance in their judgments more than extraneous outside criteria. There was, then, little evidence to support the contention that the teachers were biased in their judgments by socioeconomic factors.[2] In fact, the teachers judged their students in an instrumental manner—on the basis of institutional achievement and the absence of noticeable personality disturbances.

The MMPI profiles of students who were rated by their

[1] F. Ivan Nye, *Family Relationships and Delinquent Behavior* (New York: John Wiley and Sons, 1958), p. 155; James S. Coleman, *The Adolescent Society* (New York: The Free Press of Glencoe, 1961), chapter 2.

[2] For example see, David P. Ausubel, *Theory and Problems of Adolescent Development* (New York: Grune and Stratton, 1954), p. 334.

MMPI *Codes of Students Rated as Maladjusted*

Boys (N=22)

12'3458 9-76/0: (0:8:2:23)
1 389/476 52 0: (22:3:4:11)
21'08 47-36/59: (3:2:8:7)
2 781'49 35-6/0: (2:7:6:19)
27'80-6549/31: (4:1:11:3)
28"7'40-659/13: (0:3:8:12)
4-3 2581/79 60: (25:2:3:18)
4'689-53/17:20# (10:1:9:11)
47 2'06-531 8/9# (40:6:6:17)
4'8-1627 39/05: (17:5:1:21)
489-623 7/10:5# (2:7:3:14)
4"9382-567/10: (22:4:6:16)
4-9 60 13/28 57: (7:4:7:11)
7-52 349 618/0: (23:5:1:18)
7'80-9643/152: (15:1:11:6)
79 8'42-6 351/0: (1:5:9:13)
8"7 102 4-39 6/5: (1:2:10:10)
892'47 30-16/5# (0:8:6:17)
89 4'76-5 10 2/3: (4:0:9:9)
9"1'68 4-73 20/5: (1:2:13:5)
9 04756 238/1: (5:2:3:13)
0 47-8 29 1/36:5# (0:7:5:12)

Girls (N=12)

2 40 8-9 673/5 1: (1:2:8:9)
4"98'71-23 506/ (2:3:10:18)
6'98 4-513/720: (1:1:7:7)
60-57/23849 1: (1:3:11:9)
76 9-482301/5: (0:3:5:13)
78"13 9'24 6-5/0: (0:4:9:18)
7 86 9-24 50/13: (0:3:13:8)
9 4-6 0 387/521: (0:6:10:5)
94-78 056/23:1# (1:6:7:8)
9-572 084 / 31:6# (0:8:3:16)
9'0-7 14638/2:5# (0:7:7:8)
0-562 4/3 791:8# (0:6:7:6)

teachers as maladjusted show significant differences from those of the students rated as average or better in adjustment. Elevated profiles were more frequent among the boys rated as maladjusted and they evidenced neurotic tendencies. The maladjusted girls did not differ to any like extent when compared with their classmates who were rated as adjusted.

With respect to the validity of the teachers' ratings, it is apparent that successful academic performance and satisfactory interpersonal relations in the classroom were the primary criteria for assessing adjustment. To what extent

such behavior or performance is related to more fundamental psychiatric factors is a crucial point. Analysis of the MMPI data suggests that these levels of adjustment are interrelated and that the teachers have in their ratings identified a group of students which includes many of the potentially disturbed and deviant adolescents.

8

SUMMARY AND CONCLUSIONS

A CONSIDERABLE proportion of American youth are unable to meet the requirements of modern urban society. In the present study, the term deviancy has been employed in order to emphasize that delinquency, minority group status, low socioeconomic status, broken homes, academic failure, and maladjustment in school are important deviations from the ideal of the urban middle class white American family pattern, with its emphasis upon respectability and achievement.

The research question, then, is one of analyzing the relationship of environmental and personality factors with various types of deviant behavior among adolescents. Personality was a focal point in the study of socialization and deviance because adult behavior is largely determined by the attitudes, values, and norms internalized or accepted by the child and adolescent.

The subjects were Kentucky ninth grade public school students and incarcerated delinquents. The personality instrument used was the Minnesota Multiphasic Personality Inventory. The research design included comparisons among the students with respect to both personal and social characteristics as well as with respect to personality similarities and differences. Specifically, delinquents were compared with nondelinquents, Negroes with whites, three status levels contrasted, students from broken homes compared with those from more stable homes, three academic achievement groupings analyzed, and students rated as maladjusted by their teachers contrasted with those rated as well adjusted.

These comparisons based upon behavioral or background factors were planned before the collection of the data. Attention was directed toward those areas of the social system which were believed or known to be significant or crucial in the socialization process, such as the home or school. The background and personality differences reported among various groups, then, were not merely particular differences out of a larger context which happened to be statistically significant. Rather the plan of analysis is based upon theoretical considerations. Each of the chapters may be regarded as encompassing a separate hypothesis concerning the socialization process.

Most of the research data refers directly or indirectly to the Minnesota Multiphasic Personality Inventory. Of necessity, then, the presentation and analysis of the personality data is somewhat technical; profile and MMPI code comparisons, validity scale raw scores and mean T-scores on the clinical scales, and so forth. Therefore, an intelligent appraisal of the personality findings can only be undertaken against the background of extant MMPI research. Indeed, the present study must be viewed within this larger context

103

of previous research inasmuch as it is an outgrowth of such accumulated and expanding knowledge of personality structure and dynamics.

GENERAL FINDINGS

The general findings of the present study provide considerable substantiation of the validity of the MMPI with respect to the measurement of personality in a nonclinical adolescent population. To begin with, the mean scale scores reported for Kentucky ninth grades are quite similar to those reported in Minnesota by Hathaway and Monachesi. This outcome—corroborated for adult and clinical populations in numerous studies—supports the contention that the MMPI is tapping major dimensions of personality in nonclinical populations, and that it effects such measurement at different times and places among various types of subjects. More important, perhaps, is the validation presented in the Kentucky data with respect to nontest criteria. Thus, the overall interrelationships of behavioral and personality findings confirm—on one level—the validity of the MMPI.

The major findings with regard to delinquency support the interpretation that personality maladjustment is associated with this type of deviant behavior. The incarcerated delinquents of both sexes evidenced antisocial personality tendencies. As has been consistently reported in other studies, the delinquents scored high on the Pd scale. Personality differences between delinquents and nondelinquents were found in profile configuration (MMPI codes) as well as with respect to scale elevation.

Conversely, the MMPI profiles of the high school boys with records of delinquency were similar to those of their classmates who had not committed illegal acts. These findings prompt the interpretation that the serious and persistent offenders who frequently are incarcerated are quite different in both personality and background characteristics from boys who occasionally perpetrate minor infractions of the law. Although data is lacking on this point, it seems

104

most unlikely that the delinquency record boys will later become persistent delinquents.

The Negro students differed particularly from their white classmates in academic achievement and neurotic personality tendencies. The low scholastic performance of the Negro boys was marked; most of them were doing unsatisfactory or failing school work. Although the low socioeconomic status of the Negro students appeared to be a contributing factor to their lack of achievement motivation, this influence was either combined with other circumstances or it affected the boys and girls differently, since the Negro girls were notably superior to the Negro boys in their school achievement.

The Negro boys were characterized by neurotic tendencies—scales Hs and D. The Negro girls, on the other hand, were more introverted and sensitive in interpersonal relations. Neither group of Negro students showed evidence of aggressive personality tendencies.

Personality and behavior differences by socioeconomic status were observed. For the most part, higher status was associated with successful school performance and absence of personality maladjustment. Characteristically, the girls were having less difficulty in the adolescent socialization process than the boys. Although behavioral differences by class followed general sociological expectations, the fact that considerable variation existed within each status grouping seemed worthy of note.

Deviant or aberrant personality tendencies were more common among students from broken homes than among those from more stable homes. Especially striking was the finding that the nondelinquent boys from broken homes were characterized by depressive tendencies. The prominence of scale 2—Depression—in the codes of this group was unexpected. This finding is all the more notable when it is recalled that these boys are from a nonclinical unselected public school population. Further, scale 2 is regarded as indicative, when prominent, of serious personality difficulties.

105

Greater personality differences were evident with respect to academic achievement than was the case with respect to socioeconomic status. The girls were superior to the boys in scholastic attainment. The high achievers of both sexes were characterized by an absence of neurotic personality tendencies, while the low achievement group evidenced various personality inadequacies. As might be expected, the high achievement students had MMPI profiles which were similar to those of college students, or at least they were midway between the ordinary ninth grade profile and that of college freshmen. All in all, the data support the interpretation that academic achievement is of pervasive significance in the socialization process. Whether high achievement is the end result of a certain combination of intellectual, personality and background factors, or is itself an important influence and experience in the socialization process is uncertain. Quite likely, these influences and factors are interrelated. But it is apparent that achievement, or lack of achievement, in high school has an important impact upon both the personality and behavior of adolescents.

The teachers rated more boys than girls as "maladjusted in personality." Further, there was a definite association between the ratings and school achievement: high achievers were seldom rated as unsatisfactory in personality adjustment. Still, the MMPI data as well as the background data provided support for the efficacy of the teachers' ratings. The question of the so-called "middle-class bias" of public school teachers appears to be an over-simplification of the situation, as well as to represent a possible imputation of nefarious motives without substantiation. The teachers did in fact identify students with diverse personality configurations from various strata of society.

COMPARISON OF MMPI CODES

Perusal of the group MMPI profiles reveals a general elevation of the clinical scales above the adult norm of T-score

50. Further, it is evident that the psychotic end of the profile is markedly more elevated than the neurotic end within this adolescent population. It has been suggested that such elevation reflects the rebellion of youth. This may very well be the case. Still, it seems equally plausible within the confines of the present study to maintain that profile elevation on the MMPI reflects developmental progress or failure in the socialization process. Such failure is manifest on two levels: behavior and personality. Those boys and girls who are not successfully making their way into the adult achievement-oriented urban society give evidence of this failure by manifestations of personality aberration, or they have failed in this sense because of personality inadequacies. Existence of this reciprocal relationship between personality and behavior finds support in the research findings. It is not certain to what extent profile elevation within this or other normal adolescent populations may be considered as reflecting a rebellion against adult restraint or conventionality, or to what extent such elevation reflects developmental progress in becoming socialized. Quite likely both of these influences are operative. Some adolescents are in more or less open rebellion against adult norms, while others are slowly internalizing these same norms. Aside from the incarcerated delinquents (who in many cases have reached the point of active rebellion), it seems probable that the elevated profiles reflect the extent to which the adolescent has learned and accepted the norms of his society.

LIMITATION OF THE STUDY

Among the more apparent limitations of the study are the lack of information pertaining to adolescent social activities, including dating practices and gang behavior. Such data, if available, would have made a substantial contribution to the delineation of adolescent life here presented. In additition, the analysis and inferences are frequently based upon quite small subgroups, and the Kentucky findings may not—with regard, for example, to delinquency record boys or Negro students—obtain in other states.

A less obvious limitation of the study is that the analysis is not pursued to its logical conclusion. It is all well and good to delineate relationships between groups and note the presence or absence of significant differences. But we should also like to know why some lower status students are high achievers, why only some of the boys from broken homes are characterized by depressive tendencies, and why there are such pervasive personality and behavior differences between boys and girls who come from similar social situations. This is to say, of course, that the analysis has been concluded at the point where, it now seems, we should like it to begin.

SIGNIFICANCE OF THE STUDY

The contribution of the study is twofold. It is, first, empirical. Data pertaining to the association of personality profiles with delinquency, race, socioeconomic status, broken homes, academic achievement, educational retardation, teachers' ratings, intelligence quotient, sex, age, employment, and mobility are presented and analyzed.

The second contribution of the study is with respect to theory and method of investigation. It is maintained that the complexity of human behavior and personality necessitate research designs and analytical procedures which consider the relationship of personality to varied and complex social structures. The findings of this study provide almost compelling substantiation for the contention that specific personality variables and configurations should commonly be studied in relation to detailed background and behavioral data. Further, it is held that study of individual profiles, subgroup comparisons, and configural analysis must be undertaken if primary sources of variations are not to be ignored. To omit consideration of broken homes, intelligence, sex, race, or education of subjects poses serious limitations upon the interpretation of results. Similarly, restricting

108

a study to the analysis of a single comparison of mean profile differences may have the effect of obscuring important personality relationships. In conclusion, it is held that the present study provides detailed empirical support for the use of more varied analytical procedures and a more comprehensive theoretical orientation in the study of personality, socialization, and deviancy.

MMPI *Codes of 224 Adolescents*

Ninth Grade Boys (N=95)

12'3458 9-76/0: (0:8:2:23)
1 20-59 3/76 84: (4:3:7:8)
1 389/476 52 0: (22:3:4:11)
18'934-570/2:6# (1:4:6:13)
213 4-9786/5:0# (2:4:0:21)
2'1478 3-96/05: (9:6:7:16)
21'08 47-36/59: (3:2:8:7)
2'4 130-7 689/5: (27:6:9:11)
2-4106 3/85 79: (0:4:1:17)
26758-39 10/4: (1:4:2:18)
2'67 40-89 3/51: (0:5:3:14)
2 69-5 48 0/731: (0:2:9:8)
2 781'49 35-6/0: (2:7:6:19)
27'80-6549/31: (4:1:11:3)
2 87-35 410/96: (0:4:6:15)
287 45-60 9/13: (1:3:11:9)
28"7'40-659/13: (0:3:8:12)
34 9 56/0 128:7# (5:3:8:10)
3759 28/410 6: (17:8:4:18)
4-3 2581/79 60: (25:2:3:18)
4 37-6 182 9/50: (1:5:0:22)
456'39 2-87 1/0: (2:3:4:11)
4'689-53/17:20# (10:1:9:11)
47 2'06-531 8/9# (40:6:6:17)
47 6'52 89-3/01: (3:5:8:10)
4'8-1627 39/05: (17:5:1:21)
48"69'7 10-3/25: (5:5:12:13)
4'89-36 07/1 52: (0:4:5:20)
489-623 7/10:5# (2:7:3:14)

Ninth Grade Girls (N=105)

2 3847-159/06: (0:6:3:20)
2 40 8-9 673/51: (1:2:8:9)
31"7'8 624-9/05: (1:2:2:12)
3'1 07-846 29/5: (0:4:1:16)
34'17-6 28 90 5/ (3:9:2:21)
3-45 8 71 6/29 0: (1:4:0:24)
37-692 401/58 : (0:2:7:14)
4'18 2-70 39 56/ (0:2:10:11)
4'20-378 6/91:5# (0:3:6:9)
43-728 19/06 5: (0:9:4:21)
4 38-79 56/1 20: (0:3:1:17)
4 380/5796 12: (0:7:0:20)
4 5798 130/26: (0:4:5:17)
45-8 9073/612: (0:3:4:12)
4'637 29-81/0:5# (0:4:5:14)
4678 39/125 0: (0:2:2:15)
46'80 9-572/31: (0:3:7:6)
46 9 38-27/01:5# (2:3:4:15)
4*6'98 27-3 15/0: (0:3:8:17)
47-5 83 120/69: (4:6:3:21)
48'69 31-702/5# (4:3:9:9)
48 79-52/610 3: (0:4:6:14)
4'80-2 6793/51: (0:4:9:10)
4'9-25 80/7 136: (15:5:6:7)
49-3617 85/20: (1:8:2:18)
49386 70/251: (5:6:3:17)
4"95-68/0317 2: (8:5:3:16)
49'587-231/06: (0:8:4:19)
49'76-28 53/01: (9:5:2:15)

Ninth Grade Boys (cont.)	Ninth Grade Girls (cont.)
4-9 60 13/28 57: (7:4:7:11)	49-836 7/510 2: (2:5:7:14)
49 86 3-51 7/20: (0:5:2:20)	4"98'71-23 506/ (2:3:10:18)
5 26 9-743/081: (4:3:2:12)	5-32 9/014 78:6# (7:7:2:13)
5'6-3 90 48/27:1# (4:2:6:12)	54-60218/7 39: (0:9:12:17)
59-32648 07:1# (3:2:4:9)	54'8 627-301/9: (74:2:7:12)
59 7-8 403 6/12: (0:2:3:14)	5-4870/93 62:1# (0:5:3:14)
50-9 4678/213: (0:4:2:14)	5"9'4/768 130 2: (14:9:3:13)
69'2 87 1-3 40 5/ (2:4:11:5)	61 37 2'48-90/5: (3:5:7:18)
69-8450/732 1: (0:5:3:11)	64-891 37/2 0:5# (6:2:3:20)
7 1023 4-8 569/ (0:5:2:8)	6'40-289/57:31# (0:7:9:7)
7-52 349 618/0: (23:5:1:18)	680'5 274-91/3: (2:2:12:8)
7'80-9643/152: (15:1:11:6)	6'98 4-513/720: (1:1:7:7)
79 4'683-512/0: (7:3:4:18)	60-57/23849 1: (1:3:11:9)
79 8'42-6 351/0: (1:5:9:13)	7 25840/19 36: (12:3:2:19)
79'0 28-54/63:1# (1:4:7:4)	7-3 468 1/925 0: (9:5:5:20)
7'0 18-6 4523 9/ (8:3:10:6)	7 39 8-61 54/02: (0:4:5:15)
8 47-53 9/012:6# (11:7:5:15)	74 68-931/2 50: (0:3:3:17)
84-9 37 5/1 62 0: (0:3:4:16)	76 9-23 4 81/0:5# (1:4:1:15)
8"7 102 4-39 6/5: (1:2:10:10)	76 9-482301/5: (0:3:5:13)
87590-631/24: (3:1:1:7)	78"13 9'24 6-5/0: (0:4:9:18)
8 79 0-14 352/6: (1:5:6:13)	7'843-6 19 0/25: (1:5:1:21)
8 79'60-54/1:23# (4:3:12:6)	7 86 9-24 50/13: (0:3:13:8)
892'47 30-16/5# (0:8:6:17)	7"8 96-24 1 30/5:# (0:2:1:17)
89 4'76-5 10 2/3: (4:0:9:9)	846 7'09-52/31: (5:2:14:7)
8'97-50/14 36:2# (0:0:5:11)	84'609-721/35: (1:3:13:10)
8'05 247-1 69 3/ (8:3:11:5)	8"40 29'76-3 15/ (0:0:12:8)
9"1'68 4-73 20/5: (1:2:13:5)	8-579 34/10 2:6# (7:3:3:15)
9-258146 0/73: (13:1:4:11)	8'6 13 27-509/4: (0:3:7:8)
9 207-48 1/536: (16:1:6:9)	8"645 0-27/91:3# (2:2:11:9)
9-347 168 2/50: (6:4:3:15)	8'647902-5/13: (2:7:11:9)
9-34 8/12 76:05# (14:4:2:18)	8 69'734 15/20: (7:3:8:11)
94-35 1786/20: (11:1:2:13)	86 90 7-3 41/25: (3:2:6:5)

Ninth Grade Boys (cont.)	Ninth Grade Girls (cont.)
J'4 35-682/17 0: (21:7:4:13)	8'74-96 210/53: (0:2:3:20)
9'4/36 705:81#2 (1:2:5:10)	8"7 69'45 0-2/13: (1:0:11:10)
9'4-5 37 26/80: ' (2:3:4:10)	8-79 43/1256:0# (3:4:2:18)
94 72/50 68:1 (2:2:3:10)	89"476'0-25 13/ (0:2:12:7)
94-758/032:16# 2:6:4:12)	89 54/3 1 07:62# (14:3:3:20)
9 470-2186/3 5: (6:5:5:18)	89-6 05/7 43:21# (1:4:6:9)
9'5 34786/021: (0:1:5:9)	80-6 4793 25/1: (1:3:6:14)
95-4 267/03 18: (1:4:5:8)	9-345 802/76 1: (0:6:5:12)
9"58/406 37 1 :#2 (0:2:10:8)	9-3578 0/2164: (25:3:5:8)
9'64 5/0 38:2 17# (0:0:3:8)	9 43'7618 0-2/5: (3:4:11:11)
9"6'481-735/02: (16:5:10:20)	94 3-86 17/50:2# (0:6:3:17)
9'64-825 07/31: (7:2:11:8)	9 4-6 0 387/521: (0:6:10:5)
9'6 752-83 0/14: (52:3:7:8)	94 7-5 8 26/1 30: (0:5:6:16)
9 68 7 0-15 42/3: (4:2:13:11)	94-78 261 3/5 0: (0:7:2:22)
9'7468 3/102:5# (1:3:7:11)	9'47-86/510 23: (2:2:4:11)
9*7'84-51/3 02 6: (11:1:11:10)	94-78 056/23:1# (1:6:7:8)
9'780/2456 13: (5:3:5:10)	9"4'827-36 0/1:5# (2:5:14:6)
9'70-48 6/52:13# (1:1:8:4)	9'48/3 567012: (0:3:4:12)
9'70 8/534:16 2# (0:0:2:11)	9 48 6/73105:2# (8:3:4:19)
9-8 45 30/76:1#2 (0:2:0:12)	9*4'8 7-5 6/30 2:1# (0:1:10:7)
98'467-31 5 20/ (13:3:12:9)	95-43/67 80 2:1# (1:3:5:8)
9'854-637/12 0: (2:0:10:4)	95 48 76/310 2: (1:5:4:20)
9"87'134-56 0/2: (1:1:13:5)	9-572 084/31:6# (0:8:3:16)
98 71'45-36/20: (3:3:6:13)	964-3 78/120:5# (3:0:2:14)
9 87"46'25-103/ (1:1:7:9)	96'5 47-1 38/02: (1:3:7:16)
9 04756 238/1: (5:2:3:13)	9-6 84/570 32 1: (2:4:2:17)
0'25 7-8 43/916: (2:7:9:9)	9'7 4-6 38 1/20:5# (0:4:7:15)
0-26 5/89 47:13# (70:8:2:10)	97-680 34 1/25: (0:7:7:14)
02 76'84-3/15:9# (1:6:9:13)	9"8-43 6/70 15:2# (0:5:5:7)
0'47-5 26 8/3 19: (0:3:4:16)	9 87-605/124:3# (2:3:9:5)
0 47-8 29 1/36:5# (0:7:5:12)	98'0 274-5 36/1: (0:3:8:10)
09-47/12 6 38:5# (0:4:6:10)	9'0-7 14638/2:5# (0:7:7:8)

113

Ninth Grade Boys (cont.)	Ninth Grade Girls (cont.)

Ninth Grade Boys (cont.)

09-5 48/3 1267: (17:6:7:13)

Invalids (N=13)

4"3'82 1907-6/5: (0:2:15:6)

452-3 8791/60: (0:10:4:18)

68"9'75-4 201/3: (0:1:16:7)

8*2 679"4'13 05- (3:6:22:8)

8'6709-42 13/5: (80:6:14:5)

874*2"3'06 915- (0:5:21:8)

87*69 4"1'35-20/ (0:0:21:7)

8"76'9 52-41/30: (7:4:17:12)

8*7"9 1'024 6-35/ (0:2:30:4)

8*79641"2'30-5/ (0:1:24:7)

8*91"476'20-35/ (2:5:22:9)

98*4"7 26'3-0/15: (9:0:22:8)

9*8"704 613-52/ (41:1:16:8)

Ninth Grade Girls (cont.)

90-85 74/321 6: (2:2:7:5)

0-26 53/19 4 87: (1:3:4:9)

04-9 278 6/35:1# (0:2:5:8)

0-562 4/3 791:8# (0:6:7:6)

0-56 9/8 4723:1# (0:4:2:8)

05789-13/46 2: (25:5:9:11)

05/8 647 293:1# (0:7:1:14)

05 8-679/421 3: (2:4:7:7)

08 17-95 46 2/3: (5:4:9:10)

0-85 67/49:23 1# (0:2:9:10)

0-94/251 73 8:6# (0:4:4:10)

Invalids (N=11)

415'89-26 70 3/ (7:11:12:17)

4"8 62 901 7-53/ (0:10:3:25)

698"13450 7-2/ (0:2:21:4)

8*69 1 5'4 732-0: (9:4:33:11)

8"69'7 40-31/25: (4:1:18:5)

87'60 9-21 4 35/ (0:2:15:5)

879"6'2 314-50/ (1:5:16:8)

8913'4 20-657/ (0:8:19:12)

8*9"65 10-7 34 2/ (0:3:25:5)

8"967'4052-1/3: (2:4:22:5)

98'67 40-35 21/ (0:7:19:8)

114

INDEX

Academic achievement: comparison Ky. and Minnesota students, 85; delinquency, 7, 17, 32; environmental factors, 73, 74; high achievers compared to college students, 86, 106; personality, 79, 81, 83, 85, 86, 106; race, 39, 47, 75; sex differences, 17, 39, 55, 65, 75, 77, 79, 95, 106; socialization, 106; teachers' ratings, 99

Age: broken homes, 65; delinquent vs. nondelinquent boys, 32; juvenile delinquents in U.S., 6

Allport, G. W., 74

Altus, W. D., 83

Anonymous personality tests: undesirability, 8

Antisocial personality, 2. *See also* each MMPI scale

Ashbough, J. H., 28

Ausubel, D. P., 99

Ball, J. C., 10, 21, 30, 31, 45

Behavior patterns: establishment, 63; personality, 101

Benton, A. L., 28

Bier, W. C., 62, 85

Black, J. D., 61, 62

Block, H. A., 71

Bond, H. M., 52

Briggs, P. F., 29, 71

Broken homes: criterion, 71; delinquency, 19, 32, 63, 64; personality, 64, 67, 69, 71, 72; prevalence, 19n; race, 41, 47, 65; sex differences, 10, 69, 95

Buell, B., 52, 63, 64

Burchinal, L. G., 71

Caditz, S. B., 29

Calden, G., 48, 49

Caldwell, M. G., 29

Cannot Say score. *See* MMPI scales: ? score

Capwell, D. F., 25

Carroll, D., 10

Caste system: Negro, 37

Cayton, H. R., 35

Class ranking: threefold classification, 52, 53

Coleman, J. S., 74, 99

Correction scale. *See* MMPI scales: K score

Counts, S., 49

Cross-sectional studies: personality, 2, 35; purpose, 4, 5

Culture: delinquency, 30, 45n

D. *See* MMPI scales: Scale 2

Dahlstrom, W. G., 5, 10

Davis, J. A., 52

Davis, K., 64

Delinquency: extent in U.S., 14, 31, 32; type of offense, 21, 32; unofficial, 32
Depression. *See* MMPI scales: Scale 2
Deutsch, M., 41, 47, 48
Deviant behavior: broken homes, 63, 105; etiology, 6; noncontinuing students, 85; types, 102; urban society, 102. *See also* Delinquency, each MMPI scale, Social deviancy
Dinitz, S., 31
Dissimulation: use of K score, 11
Drake, L. E., 11

Eells, K., 53, 74
Employment: academic achievement, 77; broken homes, 67; delinquency, 17, 19, 32, 67; race, 39; socioeconomic status, 55; type of, 39, 77
Enthusiasm, 11
Erickson, M. L., 85
Erikson, E. H., 64

F score. *See* MMPI scales: F score
Family composition. *See* Broken homes
Flynn, F. T., 71
Frazier, E. F., 47

Glueck, E., 29
Glueck, S., 29
Goldfarb, W., 48
Goodenough-Anderson Scale. *See* Minnesota Scale for Parental Occupations
Goodstein, L. D., 61, 62, 83
Gough, H. G., 9, 59, 61, 83

Hathaway, S. R., 2, 8, 9, 10, 15, 25, 27, 28, 31, 61, 62, 83, 85
High MMPI scores: interpretation, 11, 62n
Hokanson, J. E., 48, 49
Hollingshead, A. B., 45, 52, 53, 74

Hovey, H. B., 62, 85
HS. *See* MMPI scales: Scale 1
Hy. *See* MMPI scales: Scale 3
Hyman, H. H., 74

Inkeles, A., 5
Intelligence, 7, 15, 17, 32, 37, 53, 65, 75, 77
Introversion. *See* MMPI: Scale 0
Invalid profiles, 8, 9, 14

Johnson, R., 29
Johnson, R. C., 29
Johnson, W. C., 83
Juvenile delinquents: academic achievement, 17, 19, 21, 32; age, 6; antisocial personality, 2; broken homes, 19, 21, 32; case history, 21; employment, 19, 32; intelligence, 15, 17, 32; personality, 27, 28, 29, 30, 104; race, 15, 32; socioeconomic status, 21, 32; subjects, 5, 6, 7, 14, 15, 31, 32, 91; teachers' ratings, 32, 91. *See also* each MMPI scale

K score. *See* MMPI scales: K score
Kahl, J. A., 52
Kardiner, A., 35, 45
Karon, B. P., 35, 48
Kausler, D. H., 83
Kay, B., 31
Klineberg, O., 35
Kodman, F., Jr., 7
Kuhlman-Anderson scale, 17

L score. *See* MMPI scales: L score
Logan, N., 21, 30
Longitudinal studies, 2
Lower class: Negro sex differences, 47; values, 52. *See also* Race, Socioeconomic level

Ma. *See* MMPI scales: Scale 9
McCary, J. L., 37
McClelland, D. C., 74
McKinley, J. C., 9, 10, 28, 62

117

MMPI, F score (continued):
ality, 97, 99; race, 41, 45;
socioeconomic level, 57, 59,
62; validity, 9
K score: academic achievement,
79; delinquency, 23, 25; description, 11; personality, 97;
school adjustment, 97; sex
differences, 41; significance,
107; socioeconomic status, 59,
62; use in study, 9; validity,
4, 5
L score: broken homes, 67; delinquency, 23, 25; description,
10; race, 45; sex differences,
41; validity, 9
Minnesota Scale for Paternal
Occupations, 19, 52
Mobility: broken homes, 65;
socioeconomic status, 53
Monachesi, E. D., 2, 15, 25, 27,
28, 31, 61, 62, 83, 85
Monahan, T. P., 15, 31
Morgan, H. H., 83
Motivation, 30
Mulligan, R. A., 52
Murphy, G., 64
Myrdal, G., 35

National Merit Scholars, 51
Nativity of subjects, 15, 53, 65
Neurotic scales. See MMPI scales
1, 2, 3
Nye, F. I., 31, 65, 99

Orlansky, H., 71
Otis Quick Scoring Mental
Abilities Test, 17
Ovesey, L., 35, 45
Owens, W. A., 83

Pa. See MMPI scales: Scale 6
Panton, J. H., 29
Parental occupations, 52n
Parsons, T., 64
Pd. See MMPI scales: Scale 4
Peck, R. F., 71
Personality: adolescents, 1, 2;
broken homes, 71, 72; de-

Personality (continued):
linquents, 27, 28, 29, 30,
104; development, 2, 63, 69;
measurement, 4, 5; study of,
2. See also each MMPI scale
Personality adjustment: academic
achievement, 81, 86, 106;
age, 93; behavior problems,
89, 91; criteria used, 99; race,
34, 35, 43, 48; rating scale
used, 88; sex differences, 69,
93, 106; socioeconomic status,
59, 62, 105; teachers' ratings,
8, 88. See also each MMPI
scale
Pt. See MMPI scales: Scale 7

Question score. See MMPI scales:
? score

Race: delinquency, 15, 32; em-
ployment, 39, 69; methodo-
logical problems, 35n; Negro
in American Society, 37, 47,
48; personality, 35, 43, 45,
48, 49, 50, 105; socioeco-
nomic status, 41, 45. See also
each MMPI scale
Randolph, M. H., 29
Reckless, W. C., 31
Redlich, F. C., 45, 52
Reiss, A. J., Jr., 31
Rempel, P. P., 29
Rhodes, A. L., 31
Richardson, H., 29
Robison, S. M., 6
Rohrer, J. H., 5

Salary: Ky. school teachers, 6
Saunders, F., 19
Sc. See MMPI scales: Scale 8
School adjustment, 93, 95, 97, 99
School districts: number in Ky., 6
Segregation: effect on academic
achievement, 47
Sherif, M., 4, 5
Shuey, A. M., 74
Si. See MMPI scales: Scale 0
Simpson, G. E., 35

118

119